Shattered Land, Unbroken Spirit- Palestine

Mario Rabi

"You don't get freedom peacefully. Freedom is never safeguarded peacefully. Anybody who is depriving you of freedom isn't deserving of a peaceful approach by the ones who are deprived of their freedom." — Malcolm X.

"A liberal is someone who opposes every war except the current war and supports all civil rights movements except the one that is going on right now." — Anonymous on X, formerly Twitter.

Fomite
Burlington, VT

All proceeds from this book will go directly to aid families in Gaza.

Fomite
58 Peru Street
Burlington, VT 05401
www.fomitepress.com

9.24/2025

To the memory of my mother and father, who supported my rebellious acts of resistance.

To Reem & Ramy so they never forget the truth of our struggle and the legacy of our land.

And to every drop of blood shed on Palestinian soil—may it water the seeds of freedom and justice.

Contents

Prologue

The pictures of a student protestor went viral the instant they were published online. Clad in black from top to bottom, hair dyed pink, and blowing a kiss to her fellow students—she was being arrested by the riot police, manhandled by three men her father's age as if she were a terrorist who had brought a gun to the campus with violent intentions. The same police who hesitated before stopping a live school shooting, who wouldn't dare mistreat a white supremacist holding up a sign calling for segregation-era laws to be reinstated, the same cops were violently crushing a peaceful protest at the Columbia University campus. It was a strange sight to behold but not something unexpected from a country where Israel calls the shots from thousands of miles across the globe.

Then another picture came into view: A young college student, probably in his twenties, in custody. The police are barely restraining themselves from throwing him to the ground and giving the White boy the type

 of treatment they usually reserve for innocent Black men walking down the street. The exposed part of the college student's underwear said, in bold white capital letters "AMERICA." A thousand words could not describe the Zionist influence over American institutions more eloquently than these simple photographs of the Columbia University protests.

What were these college students protesting? What did they want? Why were they being repressed? The poor students were oppressed by their own police—the people recruited and paid from taxpayers' money to keep Americans safe.

Next, we divert our attention to the Met Gala event, the most outrageous and shameless display of excess wealth. Hollywood celebrities—most of whom had voiced their open support for Israel and its ongoing genocide in Gaza—were the center of media attention. Mass media found it a fantastic excuse to sway people's minds from the plight of Gazans.

It was the perfect real-life interpretation of the Hunger Games, where the pictures of dying Palestinian kids and celebrities draped in designer clothes ran side by side. Everyone's social media feed was a specimen of the world's hypocrisy; one image showed a grief-stricken Palestinian father carrying the bloody, mangled corpse of his infant in his hands, looking for non-existent patches of dirt where the child could be buried, while another image showed a celebrity being carried onto the stage by two bodyguards because her dress was too tight. There was not a shadow of a doubt in people's minds after watching this contradiction that the world's mightiest nation—the self-proclaimed defenders of truth and justice—weren't just indifferent to the plight of Palestinians; they were actively causing it.

But the world's hypocrisy and double standards about Israel were most apparent from Eurovision, the competition that barred Russian vocalists from participating in 2022 due to the crisis in Ukraine but let Israeli songwriters perform on the big stage. Eden Golan performed her genocidal song despite thousands of spectators trying to boo her off the stage.

Peaceful protesters with Palestinian flags outside the venue were disrupted by police. The slur "antisemitism" was used to describe peaceful protestors who only wanted Israel to stop massacring Palestinian children and dropping the fury of hell over them under the guise of "luring out Hamas leaders." The same world that was ready to boycott Russian celebrities, tourists, athletes, and even innocent citizens who had nothing to do with Putin's policies—these same entities are now defending the heinous crimes of the ultra-fascist, ethno-nationalist Zionist regime, calling it self-defense.

But the Palestinian dream won't be so easily forgotten; the whole world is slowly realizing that Hamas isn't the problem: Zionism is. This isn't a war between Islam and Christianity or Islam and Judaism; it is simply a nation's struggle to throw away the yoke of slavery and regain their freedom.

As Hamas clearly explained in their rewritten charter, their battle is for freedom, for struggle, for the right to return to their lands from where their forefathers were driven away by people from Europe and Russia who believed that their ancestry and race gave them the right to steal other people's lands.

> *"It means that we don't fight Jews because they are Jews. Our struggle is only against those who occupied our lands." — Taher al-Nounou.*

Today, Zionists can buy everyone; they can buy the whole wide world. Politicians are paid by the AIPAC, and celebrities are coerced into supporting Israel under the threat of losing their jobs. Journalists can be bought by promises of real estate opportunities in New Gaza. Public figures like Elon Musk can be made to aid the Zionist regime with a few dog tags. But no one can stop everyday citizens, students, and working men and women from standing up in favor of Palestine.

The Palestinian dream is now more alive than ever before. For every child that Israel massacres in the West Bank, ten people in America convert to the cause of the liberation of Palestine. "Free Palestine" has become the new "Black Lives Matter." It garnered support from African Americans, the Irish, the "woke" students, and Muslims from all over the world.

In the following chapters, you'll learn the true story of Palestine, unadulterated, unabashed, and free from the lies peddled by the Jewish lobby in the mass media. You'll learn the racist and ethno-nationalist past of the whole Zionist movement. Together, we'll explore how Christian and Muslim, residents of Palestine were the first to raise objections against the infiltration of Zionists in their ancestral homeland. You'll see how Christians, Muslims and Jews lived in harmony in the Holy Land before they were disrupted by White Europeans who divided them in the name of religion and stole the land where Palestinians had been living, not for centuries, but for millennia.

If you want to know the cause of the October Seven event and wish to learn the very valid reasons for Hamas's resistance of Israel, then continue reading this book. You'll soon understand why Zionism is the root cause of violence, not just in Gaza or the West Bank, but in the entire Middle East.

What is Palestine? Is it merely a piece of land covering 6,025 square kilometers and holding 5,466,981 people driven away from their ancestral lands? Or is it also a nation that has faced apartheid in the past and is facing genocide in the present, a hotbed of regional conflict often ignored by Western countries? Is it history repeating itself and reminding us of when the West ignored Nazi Germany's atrocities?

The issue of Palestine has always been a topic of hot debate and hush-hush conversations in the West. As Israel's influence on Western civilization continues to grow, the Zionist regime's allies keep averting their eyes from an ongoing conflict that has always had the potential to lead to genocide.

So, what's the root cause of today's humanitarian crisis in the Holy Land? What has led to the current genocide of the Gazans? For that, we must journey back in time and closely examine the history of Palestine, its land, and its people.

Palestine holds immense religious significance for Abraham and his descendants. Jerusalem, or *Al-Quds*, stands as a testament to this rich history. Coveted throughout human history, the city has endured attacks, pillaging, and rule by various civilizations— Christians, and Muslims alike.

If we talk about Christianity, Bethlehem, Nazareth, and Jerusalem are pivotal to the Christian faith and attract millions of pilgrims annually. The Church of the Holy Sepulchre is believed to be the site of Jesus's crucifixion and resurrection. For Muslims, Palestine holds deep religious significance as their first *Qibla*, where they directed their faces while worshiping before the Holy Mosque in Mecca was made the new *Qibla*.

To this day, Jerusalem remains the third holiest site in Islam after the two holy cities of Mecca and Medina. Located on *Haram al-Sharif* in Jerusalem, the Al-Aqsa Mosque is revered by every Muslim as the place where Prophet Muhammad ascended to the heavens during the Night Journey (*Isra* and *Mi'raj*).

It seems that Palestine is considered the sacred land for three of the world's major religions. But, rather than acknowledge and respect this fact, Israel has seized this opportunity to run a colonizing scheme and wipe out generations of Palestinians who have inhabited their homeland for decades. However, Israel's colonizing and genocidal strategies are not something that came into being overnight but have been brewing since the 1800s.

Following the conquest of Jerusalem in 1516, Palestinians had been living under the peaceful leadership of the Ottomans. The early 1840s were a time when the European nations were grabbing every little piece of land they could conquer, and the Middle East was being eyed as a means for spreading this colonial influence to the Arab world.

The idea of a Zionist regime in Palestine was proposed by wealthy Jews who had founded business empires in Europe and America in the 1850s. By the 1890s, Jews had started buying patches of land in Palestine, but the Ottoman Empire kept a watchful eye over those purchases and would not allow the local population to be displaced by Jewish immigrants from Europe.

However, it wasn't until World War I that the British, who were fighting the Ottomans, showed their support for the idea of a Jewish state in the region. It helped them garner the support of Jewish millionaires. Support for a Jewish homeland in Palestine intensified after the rise in antisemitism, persecution, and hostility toward the Jews in Nazi Germany in the 1930s. The Jews were on the lookout for a state that would welcome their displaced population with open arms. This was the precise moment that the Zionists proposed the land of Palestine as the perfect place for occupation.

Historical reports show that the early Zionists were aware of how much the local population, the Palestinians- would detest the occupation of their homeland and the influx of White foreigners into their ancestral lands. However, Zionists were adamant about conquering Palestine and establishing a Jewish homeland there.

As you continue reading this book, you'll realize that the grossly unjust struggle is not new. Rather, it has been fueled by years of illegal settlements, the sheer resentment among the Israelis for Palestinians, and a recent call to take over the Gaza Strip and displace more than two million Palestinians by force. The Gaza Strip is a narrow piece of land that came under the occupation of Israel after the Six-Day War in 1967. Since then, Gaza has been a focal point of the Israeli-Palestinian conflict, characterized by ongoing tensions, violence, and humanitarian crises.

But this is just the beginning of our story, the story of Gaza and its reawakening. In the next chapters, you will realize why the October Seven event took place and how it was used as an excuse by the fascist Israeli government to steal yet more of the land in Palestine, land that they had not yet occupied.

1. History of Gazans and Palestine

In the alleyways of Shatila, there lies a dark corner that one can't reach without navigating the slums and ghettos of southern Beirut. In this corner, Mohamed Issi Khatib built a small sanctuary that he calls his "Museum of Memory" (Fisk, 2018), containing artifacts from the Palestinian village of al-Khalisa, where his ancestors had been living for centuries, only to be driven away by the Jewish forces in 1948.

Khatib has adorned this small museum with ancient farm scythes that his forefathers used. They had been farmers when there was peace and harmony in the land of Palestine, and they lived in their modest but beautiful houses made of black basalt stones.

His shabby museum also contains old radio sets from the forties, brass coffee pots made, land deeds going back to the time of the Ottoman Empire, and—Khatib's most cherished possession—the keys to a house he's never seen in his life. The same house that his parents saw for the last time on May 11, 1948, when the Hagenah militia forced the villagers to escape to bordering Lebanon, never again to return to the patch of Earth where their ancestors' bones were resting.

These three keys were old and rusted—one was withered, almost as if it were hundreds of years old. But it reminds Khatib of his parents' suffering. He can't see the house from Shatila. However, if he travels to the southernmost part of Lebanon and looks past the border fence toward the land which is now the Israeli city of Kiryat Shmona, he can still see the land which rightfully belongs to his forefathers. The keys in his museum never let him forget that it is his destiny to one day return to his roots and reclaim the stolen land from the Zionists.

Khatib is just one of many Palestinians who still hold on dearly to the houses their parents lived in, or that they themselves lived in as kids before the events of the 1940s when they were forcefully driven away from their homes by Zionist barbarians, who believed that, due to their White privilege, they had more right to the sacred land of Palestine than the Palestinians.

However, we can't properly understand the sufferings of Palestinians without dropping our buckets deep into the wells of history and trying to scrape up the fundamentals of the history of Palestine. Digging deep into the annals of Gazan history will allow us to understand better the folly of the Zionist schemes and the weaknesses of their arguments. A historical analysis of the history of Palestine is necessary to understand the crimes Israelis have committed—and are still committing unabashedly in front of the whole world—against Gazans. We will learn who the *actual* inhabitants of Palestine are and how European immigrants currently occupying the Holy Land have misrepresented themselves. Palestine's true sons of the soil are the Muslim, Christian, and Jewish natives who have been living on this land for the past not hundreds but *thousands* of years.

Ancient Civilizations: Phoenicians, Egyptians, and Canaanites

Long before the first bricks of Judaism were laid, before Abraham or the other patriarchs were born, the land of Palestine was thriving under a different name. Palestine, particularly the region of Gaza, has long been inhabited by great civilizations. The earliest settlements in Gaza date back to over 5,000 years ago, and the remnants of these ancient Gazans are still to be found in places like Tell es-Sakan.

During the Bronze Age, many small agricultural settlements were scattered all over Gaza. These settlements show how Gazans were involved in commercial activities in the Mediterranean region and the Middle East. Agricultural and maritime trade was booming in Gaza, and this patch of land served as a critical strategic location in West Asia. That's why Gaza—not unlike the trade-rich country of Yemen—has always been the focus of attention from major civilizations. From Canaanites and Phoenicians to Egyptians—this land was coveted by all civilizations for its status as a major commercial hub.

We'll introduce you to the major civilizations that contributed to the development of this beautiful region as well as its culture and civilization. First, this rich and diverse land was inhabited by Canaanites, who are regarded as the pioneering forefathers of native Palestinians. They were known for their seafaring skills.

Their descendants, the Phoenicians, contributed not only to the region's economic development but also created alphabets and laid the foundations of the modern writing system. Slowly, their civilization spread to North Africa, taking over all major maritime trade routes in the Mediterranean Sea and threatening the economic monopoly of the Roman Empire.

Egyptians and Palestinians were involved in mutually beneficial commercial activities as early as the fourth millennium BCE. However, the Pharaohs conquered and annexed Palestine around 1,500 years before the birth of Christ. In the late Bronze Age, the region of Gaza was under Egyptian occupation. Then, in the twelfth century BCE, the Philistines finally arrived in Palestine.

Today, the region's religious significance, particularly that of the city of Jerusalem—has served as the sacred place of worship in all of the Abrahamic religions.

Jerusalem's importance as a holy city for multiple faiths underscores the region's enduring cultural and religious heritage, shaping the identities of those who have called Palestine home over the centuries. But it also leads to religious violence, often erupting in genocide, like the one being carried out in Gaza as of this writing. If we are to understand the proper history of Gaza, we must go deeper into the historical truths about who the land of Palestine really belongs to.

Palestine of its original inhabitants, a goal they have started to pursue more actively (and publicly) since the events of October Seven.

The Beginning of the Christian Rule

In the fourth century CE, Roman emperor Constantine I embraced Christianity. It started a new chapter in the history of Palestine. The whole region became an important center of Christian teachings. It started attracting monks, scholars, orators, pilgrims, etc., from all over the world. This period lasted for the next three centuries and ended when Muslims conquered Palestine in the seventh century.

Palestine in the Age of Islam

The city of Jerusalem was the first *Qiblah* of Muslims and was eventually annexed to the expanding Rashidun Caliphate in the era of Caliph Umar I. It remained an important province of the Islamic Empire under the Umayyads, Abbasids, Tulunids, Ikhshidids, and Fatimids. The Umayyads elevated it to a new height when the seat of the Caliphate was moved from Kufah to Damascus, less than 200 miles from Jerusalem.

Muslims constructed the Dome of the Rock and the al-Aqsa Mosque in the holy city, and an era of distinctly Arab heritage prospered in Palestine. However, the Muslim rule came to a brief pause after more than three centuries when the Crusaders conquered Jerusalem in 1099 CE. At the behest of Pope Urban II, the Crusaders marched across Europe, massacring Jews and Muslims along the way, until they reached the Levant and conquered the city. But they were not destined to remain there for long.

From the Ayyubids to the Ottomans

The Christian-ruled Jerusalem disintegrated in 1187 CE when Salah-

Eddine retook the holy city in the name of Islam. The land of Palestine continued to serve as a province maintained firstly, by the Ayyubids, and then by the Ma]mluks, who primarily ruled the Levant from their Egypt-based sultanates. The Ayyubids had taken the rich and fertile lands of the Nile from the Shia Fatimid dynasty. However, as the power of the Mamluks waned, the entire land of Palestine suffered an economic decline, as well as the ravages of several epidemics.

But the natives were resilient, and they continued to thrive. In the early years of the sixteenth century, Palestine came under Ottoman rule. Selim I, the first Ottoman emperor to declare his Caliphate, defeated the Mamluk vassals in 1516 CE and took over the administration of Jerusalem. As the father of Suleiman the Magnificent, Selim I is regarded as one of the most successful emperors in the Ottoman dynasty. From 1516 to 1918, Palestine remained in the custody of the Ottoman Caliphs (except for a period in the 1830s when Egyptians managed to conquer the Holy Land).

Let's explore the Ottoman rule in more detail and see how it affected the future of the local community when the Ottoman Empire was defeated in WWI, and the Zionist scheme to overthrow their Ottoman benefactors came to fruition.

2. Ottoman Rule and the British Mandate

"I won't sell anything, not even an inch of this territory, because this country does not belong to me but to all Ottomans. My people won these lands with their blood. We give what we have the way we got it in the first place." — *The Ottoman Sultan.*

In the summer of 1901, Philip Newlinsky appeared in the court of Sultan Abdulhamid II with an offer from Budapest native Theodor Herzl, the covetous Jew who founded the Zionist movement. It was a seemingly simple request: Herzel wanted the Sultan to open the sacred land of Palestine to Jewish settlers from Europe and Russia so they could start administering this region and replace the natives. As a reward, they offered to pay foreign debts and even help the Sultan gain popularity among Europeans with the tools the Hebrew nation is most famous for: propaganda.

However, the Sultan refused this *generous* request draped in benevolence to cover the ill intentions of the father of global Zionism by uttering the words quoted above. This glorious scene was beautifully recreated by the showrunners of the famous Turkish drama series *Payitaht*, airing between 2017 and 2021 on TRT. The Sultan was a protector of the land of Gaza and a defender of the rights of the native people of Palestine to rule their *own* land, just like his predecessors, the noble sultans of the Ottoman Dynasty.

The Ottoman period was an era of peace and stability in the region. Gaza became a major administrative hub and played a crucial role in the Ottoman Empire history. In this chapter, we'll explore Gaza under the suzerainty of Ottomans and the transition to a British mandate. It'll set the stage for discussing the Gaza Genocide and how the Zionists succeeded in conquering this patch of land by sheer malice and treachery.

Palestine under Ottoman Rule

The Ottomans conquered Gaza in 1517 and integrated it into the province of Syria. It became a part of the *sanjak* of Jerusalem that was part of the *vilayet* of Damascus. But Gaza didn't just change owners in 1517 when the Ottomans took over; it also experienced a period of significant bureaucratic changes. The Ottomans changed the outdated taxation system and introduced new government institutions. The land registration system of *Tapu* formalized land ownership in Gaza.

But the Gazans didn't lose their autonomy. While the Ottomans were the ultimate authority in civil and legal matters, local nobles were autonomous in some levels of decision-making. So, how did the Ottoman rule affect the Gazan environment and what were the long-lasting effects on its culture?

Social and Economic Stability

The Ottoman rule was a period of social stability and economic progress for native Palestinians. The tiny patch of land called Gaza has always been a major trading hub. History says that Hashim, the patriarch of the famous *Banu Hashim* clan and the great-grandfather of the Prophet Muhammad, died in Gaza while on a business trip, and a grave in the city is still attributed to him.

In the Ottoman period, Gaza connected the trade routes coming from Egypt, the Levant, and Arabia. The markets of G]aza thronged with products like spices, textiles, and grains. The Ottomans wanted Gaza to prosper, so they built roads and *caravanserais* (inns) to foster trade caravans throughout the whole region.

The Ottomans also promoted better land cultivation policies and irrigation projects. Olives, barley, etc., became the major local produce in Gaza between the sixteenth and twentieth centuries. Maritime trade in Gaza also prospered and reached new heights under the watchful gaze of Ottomans. Under the Ridwan Dynasty (which had a stronghold in Gaza until 1690 CE), Gaza transformed from an inactive port to a major trading hub. It contributed heavily to the religious and cultural enrichment of the natives.

Religious and Cultural Aspects of the Ottoman Rule

At the beginning of the ongoing genocide, children (those under eighteen) comprised over half of the Palestinian population (Nassar, n.d.). The country, now illegally known as "Israel," once had a majority Arab population. Unlike today, the Palestine of the Ottoman era was a Muslim-dominant region devoid of a significant European population. For example, the graph below shows how the Gazan population demographics changed between 1872 and 1948.

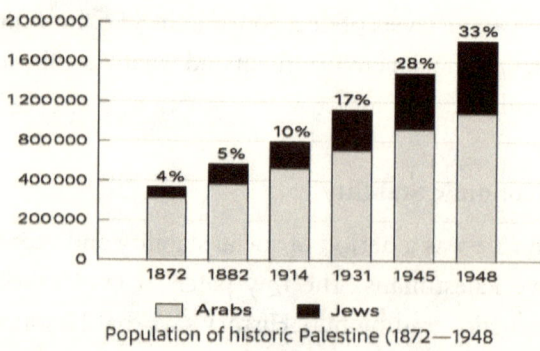

Population of historic Palestine (1872—1948

You can see that Jews made up 4 percent of the local population. These numbers include the local Jewry as well, which was on friendly terms with the Muslim and Christian population.

Under the *Tanzimat* reforms, Jews were allowed to settle in Palestine. As a result, the Jewish population in Gaza more than doubled between 1840 and 1880. But you can see that it only managed to reach a mere 10 percent when the Ottomans were breathing their last, and Turkey had become the "Weak Man of Europe." However, the Ottomans controlled the population growth of foreigners in Palestine; they prevented a population inversion in which immigrants slowly outnumbered the locals. By this means, the Ottomans protected the cultural and religious identity of the native Palestinians. They ensured the port of Gaza remained predominantly Muslim. A sizable number of Christians were permitted to openly practice their religion in Palestine. There were Druze, Jews, and other groups as well. In short, the Ottomans assumed a pluralistic approach toward governing Gaza.

Moreover, they oversaw the building and reconstruction of several local mosques and *madrassahs* (small religious schools). Sufi lodges received state funding, while the Sultans patronized arts and architecture in the city. They were patrons of poetry and writing as well. Sadly, many structures that were kept intact by the Ottomans were later attacked and destroyed by Zionists in their bloody, murderous, and vindictive rampage in Gaza.

The Balfour Declaration - A Promise Built on Betrayal

Foreign Office,
November 2nd, 1917.

Dear Lord Rothschild,

I have much pleasure in conveying to you, on behalf of His Majesty's Government, the following declaration of sympathy with Jewish Zionist aspirations which has been submitted to, and approved by, the Cabinet

"His Majesty's Government view with favour the establishment in Palestine of a national home for the Jewish people, and will use their best endeavours to facilitate the achievement of this object, it being clearly understood that nothing shall be done which may prejudice the civil and religious rights of existing non-Jewish communities in Palestine, or the rights and political status enjoyed by Jews in any other country"

I should be grateful if you would bring this declaration to the knowledge of the Zionist Federation.

November 2, 1917. A single letter, seventy-six words long, sealed the fate of an entire people. Drafted in the heart of the British Empire and signed by Foreign Secretary Arthur Balfour, it was a declaration that would forever alter the land of Palestine. At first glance, the letter appears to strike a balance—a commitment to establishing a "national home for the Jewish people" while vowing that "nothing shall be done" to harm the rights of Palestine's existing inhabitants. But beneath the diplomatic wording lies a contradiction so vast, so deliberate, that it can only be described as a masterclass in imperial deception.

This was not Britain's only betrayal. Two years earlier, in secret correspondence with Sharif Hussein of Mecca, the British had dangled the prospect of Arab independence in exchange for an uprising against the Ottomans. Palestine, the Arabs were told, would be theirs. That lie had barely settled before Britain inked another backroom deal—the Sykes-Picot Agreement—carving up the Middle East with France as if drawing lines on a blank map. The Balfour Declaration was simply the final piece of this colonial chess game, sacrificing an entire people in service of European geopolitics.

And so, with a single stroke of a pen, Balfour set in motion a century of displacement, war, and resistance. A declaration not of sympathy, but of erasure. A promise built not on justice, but on betrayal.

The Great Deception

The Balfour Declaration was not just a letter—it was an imperial weapon, a document laced with contradictions that would reshape history. Under the guise of diplomacy, Britain issued a promise that defied logic, law, and morality. A promise built on illusion, contradiction, and betrayal.

A Land Promised Twice

In 1917, Britain had no legal claim to Palestine. The land was still under Ottoman rule, yet the British government took it upon itself to pledge what it did not own. With one hand, Britain carved out a "national home" for the Jewish people; with the other, it vowed to protect the rights of Palestine's existing population. But what happens when one promise cannot exist without erasing the other?

The Balancing Act That Never Was

To Zionists: The declaration offered support for a Jewish homeland.

To Arabs: It gave assurances that their rights would remain untouched.

But words on paper do not change reality. In 1917, Arabs made up the overwhelming majority in Palestine. A homeland for people on land already inhabited by another—how could Britain resolve this contradiction? The answer was simple: it couldn't. It never intended to!

The Empty Shell of a 'National Home'

The phrase "national home" was deliberately vague, a masterpiece of ambiguity. Did it mean statehood? Limited autonomy? A symbolic presence? The British left the term undefined, giving themselves room to maneuver while ensuring both Zionists and Arabs could interpret it as they wished—until reality proved otherwise.

The British Empire was not in the business of keeping promises; it was in the business of conquest.

Palestinians—Erased Before the Ink Dried

The declaration spoke of Jewish aspirations. It spoke of safeguarding non-Jewish "civil and religious" rights. But nowhere did it acknowledge Palestinian **political** rights—because to do so would have been to admit their sovereignty. Britain ensured that the native population of Palestine was nothing more than an afterthought in their own land.

History's Unfolding Tragedy

A letter written in London set fire to the Middle East. It was not a gesture of goodwill but a calculated act of imperial strategy, one that disregarded the people of Palestine, divided the region, and paved the way for decades of dispossession, resistance, and bloodshed. The Balfour Declaration did not create peace; it institutionalized conflict. A century later, its shadow still looms.

The Balfour Letter, written by Lord Balfour to the immensely wealthy Rothschild, was one of the catalysts for the ongoing genocide of Palestinians.

Palestine, under the British Mandate

The collapse of the Ottoman Empire is a topic that requires careful investigation. Historians disagree about when it actually started. It is commonly argued that the seventeenth century was when the Ottoman Dynasty started losing power and influence, lacking, as they did, the more sophisticated weaponry and resources of their rivals. It was an era of depravity and corruption; weak sultans ruled Turkey, and most of them were just as powerful as the last few Abbasid Caliphs.

After WWI, however, the great and mighty Ottoman Empire disintegrated. The Treaty of Sevres in 1920 was a significant blow to the power and influence of the Ottoman Caliphate (*Khilafat-e-Uthmaniyah*). The Treaty of Lausanne in 1923 led to the dismantling of the Empire and Gaza, which came under the British mandate. It was a League of Nation's mandate, but in reality, the British were calling the shots. And, as per the Balfour Declaration, they wished to bestow upon the global Jewry the sacred land of Palestine.

Let's review some of the key changes taking place under the British mandate and how they forever transformed the religious/cultural lives of the natives. The consequences of letting Europeans settle there were grave in the extreme. Ultimately, this mandate precipitated a 75-year-long cycle of violence and bloodshed.

Administrative Changes

The British reorganized Gaza administratively. The United Kingdom authorities established a Civil Administration of Palestine. Jerusalem served as its headquarters, while Gaza joined the southern district of this entity. The British colonial policies affected how local governance was structured. Even though the British brought an era of modernity to Gaza, they ignored local laws and traditions. As a result, the Gazan lifestyle was severely affected, leading to major social/cultural shifts.

Social and Economic Changes

The British constructed more roads in Gaza and laid down railway lines. These measures facilitated trade and mobility in the region. However, these moves primarily served British interests, and the local population of Gaza couldn't benefit significantly from these infrastructural improvements.

> "In the 1920s, during the first decade of the British Mandate, Palestine's agricultural sector did not fare well except for plantation and cash crops such as citrus and bananas. In the early 1930s, before the peasants suffered five consecutive years of poor crop yields, many villagers were disillusioned by their financial difficulties; they were no longer making efforts to extricate themselves from their indebtedness to the government and moneylenders." — Kenneth W. Stein.

The curse of Jewish dominance and land ownership conflicts were another source of discomfort for locals who saw sudden changes in the agricultural sector. Modern agricultural trends in Gaza benefited only the major landowners, while small landowners and farmers struggled.

Urbanization played a crucial role in transforming the centuries-old lifestyle of Gazans. The social fabric of Palestine was rapidly changing in the post-WWI era. It brings us to a discussion on the impact of colonialism in Palestine.

How did Colonialism Impact Gaza?

I would like to explore two aspects of the impact of colonialism on an average Palestinian's life.

Regional Tensions due to British Policies: The era of British mandate saw increased tensions between locals (Arabs) and foreigners (Jews). When the Balfour Declaration openly expressed the Crown's support for the creation of a "national home for the Jewish people," it naturally made Palestinians furious over how unfairly their white oppressors could distribute their ancestral lands between foreign settlers. The influx of Jews was a major problem since it displaced the local farmers, heightening economic disparities. The 2nd, 3rd, 4th, and 4th *Aliyah* alone collectively saw the arrival of more than 400,000 Jewish immigrants in Palestine. This move accelerated the rise of Palestinian self-determination. Both Muslims and Christians native to Palestine were actively speaking against this injustice and criticizing the British government for displacing the local Arab population.

Social and Cultural Transformations: The British didn't just replace Palestinians or give Jews free rein in Gaza; they also transformed the region's entire educational system, precisely the same thing that happened to Indian Muslims. These institutions were established under the impression that they would modernize Palestinians but also had a hidden objective to promote Western values that were often in contrast with the local Islamic traditions. This duality created a lot of tension in the region when Palestinians refused to fully adapt to these new norms that were being imposed upon them—Muslims and non-Muslims alike. The Zionist movement wasn't the only movement thriving in Palestine, thanks to the unlimited funding and support of Western Jewry and the British government; the rise of Arab nationalism created polarized identities in Palestine. The success of Slavic and Balkan nationalist movements piqued Arabs' curiosity about the prospects of winning their freedom. Many Palestinians were affected by the wave of Arab nationalism.

Next, we'll take a deeper look at how WWI and the Balfour Declaration affected the Gazan lifestyle.

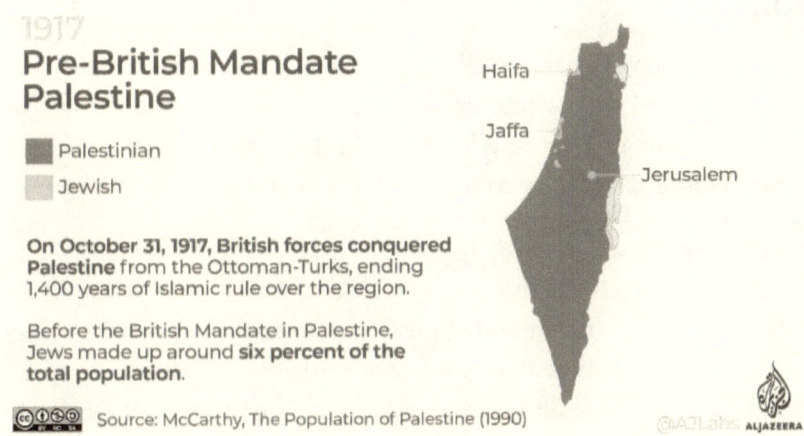

Pre-British Mandate Palestine

Haifa

Jaffa

Jerusalem

■ Palestinian

■ Jewish

On October 31, 1917, British forces conquered Palestine from the Ottoman-Turks, ending 1,400 years of Islamic rule over the region.

Before the British Mandate in Palestine, Jews made up around **six percent of the total population**.

Source: McCarthy, The Population of Palestine (1990)

@AJLabs ALJAZEERA

Balfour Declaration: The Hebrew Nation's Contract with the Devil

The turning point came in 1917 with the historic Balfour Declaration—a letter bearing Britain's support for a "national home for the Jewish people" in Palestine. For Zionists, this declaration was nothing short of a triumph, a beacon of hope in their quest for self-determination and safety amidst growing antisemitism in Europe.

As you can see in the demographic, Palestinians were in a whopping majority, and Jews made up less than 6 percent of the total population of Jerusalem (Haddad & Chughtai, 2023).

Amidst the political maneuvering and diplomatic intricacies, real lives were impacted. Hundreds of families living across Europe faced the harsh realities of persecution and sought refuge in a distant land they called their own. The promise of a homeland in Palestine beckoned, and waves of Jewish migrants set out on journeys fraught with hope and uncertainty. As Jewish communities flourished in Palestine, their growing presence sparked tensions among the indigenous and rightful Palestinian population. The 1930s witnessed mounting apprehensions and discontent, culminating in the Palestinian revolt from 1936 to 1939—a poignant expression of resistance against perceived threats to their homeland and identity.

WWI: A Deep Dive into the Annals of the Mid-Twentieth-Century Palestine

The effects of WWI and WWII were far-reaching; while the Second World War led to the foundation of the Jewish "homeland" in the ancestral lands of Palestinian Arabs, the First World War weakened the frail Ottoman Empire to such a great extent that it couldn't recover from Ataturk's influence.

General Edmund Allenby captured Gaza in 1917, and later, the Sykes-Picot Agreement divided the Ottoman territories that rightfully belonged to the people living on these lands between their European conquerors who divided these lands on the map without regard to local customs and traditions.

It's said that most of the regional and international conflicts in Asia and Africa are caused by the British's poor mapping and division of territories. This created the Kashmir conflict between India and Pakistan; an even worse (and more malicious) British mapping endeavor in Palestine that eventually led to an ongoing genocide in which over 100,000 Palestinians have been killed, missing, or wounded at the hands of the IDF soldiers.

The Seeds of Conflict: The Balfour Declaration was very ambiguous as it both promised Jews a homeland in Palestine but also asserted that the locals wouldn't face any injustice. But the Jewry were pleased about this promise as it galvanized the Zionist movement. Secular Zionists, who sought a Jewish homeland in Africa and would have likely settled for Madagascar as a sovereign Jewish nation, were seduced by the Balfour Declaration to immigrate to Palestine and disrupt the peace in this region. Jewish settlers established *kibbutzim* or agricultural communities that sowed the initial seeds of conflict between them and the native Arabs, who rightfully felt marginalized and dispossessed by a sudden influx of thousands of foreigners into their ancestral lands.

The Conflict Erupts: As ever, the British couldn't successfully resolve the conflicts arising between locals and immigrants. Economic disparities kept rising, and political grievances merely intensified. Violent clashes took place between the 1920s and 1930s, including the Jaffa riots of 1921 and the Hebron riots of 1929.

The Idea of Partition: The 1930s were an era of poor governance in Palestine. The Arab Revolt (1936-1939) also demonstrated that the British government had failed to address the grievances of the local populace and couldn't limit the influx of Jews from Russia or Europe into Palestine. The Arabs were clearly seeing the big picture; it was an unholy attempt to usurp their ancestral lands and give it all to foreigners. The British were now unable to surrender to the Jewish population's unfair demands. The Peel Commission suggested in 1937 that Palestine must be divided into Arab and Jewish regions; however, this proposal was fiercely rejected by Arabs and Jews. In 1939, a White Paper proposed limiting the influx of Jewish migrants into Palestine. This, too, was met with fierce opposition from Zionist leaders.

The UN Partition Plan: The Final Nail in the Coffin of Palestine Sovereignty

Meet the aftermath of World War II, a time of great change and hope but also deep-seated tensions in Palestine. After years of conflict between Arabs and Jews over land and rights, Britain, which had control over Palestine, decided it was time to step back. They asked the United Nations (UN), a global organization formed after the war to promote peace, to help figure out what to do next.

By the end of 1946, there were about 1.3 million Arabs and over 600,000 Jews in Palestine. Then, in 1947, something big happened. The UN members voted on a plan to split Palestine into two separate countries—one for Jews and one for Arabs. The idea was to give each group their own place to govern and live in peace. But this plan was rooted in malice and the desire to swindle Arabs of their legally owned land, much like the way in which the settlers from Europe dishonestly bought Native American lands.

The plan also said that important places like Jerusalem and Bethlehem would be managed by an international group because they were sacred to different religions. Many Jewish leaders were happy with the plan because it gave them a chance to have their own country after years of struggle. However, Palestinian Arabs and nearby Arab countries felt betrayed. They believed the plan gave too much land to the Jews and didn't respect the rights of the Arab Palestinians who had been living there for generations.

Tensions quickly boiled over. Just days after the UN vote, fighting broke out between Arab and Jewish communities in Palestine. The dream of peaceful coexistence seemed farther away than ever. Behind these monumental decisions were real people—families worried about their homes and futures, neighbors suddenly finding themselves on different sides of a new border, and communities grappling with fear and uncertainty about what the future held. The UN's plan was supposed to bring peace, but it ended up sparking more conflict and heartache for many people caught in the middle of a complex struggle for land and identity.

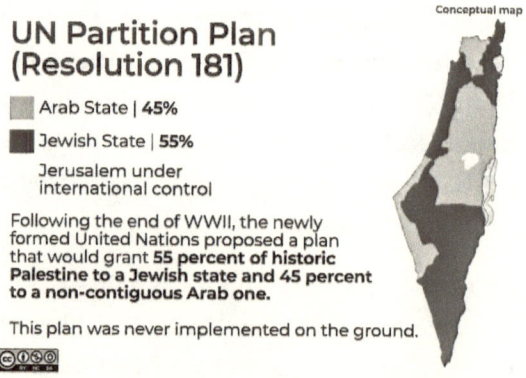

UN Partition Plan (Resolution 181)

Arab State | **45%**

Jewish State | **55%**

Jerusalem under international control

Following the end of WWII, the newly formed United Nations proposed a plan that would grant **55 percent of historic Palestine to a Jewish state and 45 percent to a non-contiguous Arab one.**

This plan was never implemented on the ground.

Conceptual map

(Haddad & Chughtai, 2023b)

This was a brief history of the land of Palestine from the era of the Ottomans to the establishment of the British mandate. In the next chapter, we'll discuss the event known as the Nakbah and respond to some of the most popular misconceptions Zionists spread regarding it.

What's happening in Palestine right now is only a repetition of the Nakbah, in which Jews burnt and beheaded Arab babies. Now, you'll see how the Nakbah isn't over; it's a continuous series of oppression that every Palestinian faces in Israel every single day.

3. The Nakbah and the Birth of Israel

"If I were an Arab leader, I'd never sign an agreement with Israel. It's normal; we have taken their country. It's true; God promised it to us. But how could that interest them? Our God isn't theirs. There has been Antisemitism, the Nazis, Hitler, Auschwitz, but was that their fault? They see but one thing: we have come, and we have stolen their country. Why would they accept that?" — David Ben-Gurion, quoted in Nahum Goldmann's The Jewish Paradox.

The Gaza Genocide began in October 2023, and out came the defenders of Zionism from their tunnels, starkly resembling the Hasidic Jews who were caught red-handed indulging in brutish rituals in the subways and undergrounds of NYC (McCausland, 2024). Many supporters of Israel argued that the "Palestinian identity" was made up and didn't exist before the events of Nakbah. Palestinian activists quickly shared the pictures of the bronze 1 Mil coin minted by the British Mandate in 1927. This coin depicts an olive branch with the word "Palestine" written in both English and Arabic. In the parentheses, one can barely make out the acronym "The Land of Israel" in Hebrew, indicating the British overseer's plan to create a national home for the Hebrew people in the ancestral lands of Palestinians.

Even though the olive branch represented peace between Arabs and Jews, practically, the Crown's policy was to placate the Jews and allow them to usurp as much territory in Palestine as possible. In the face of rising Jewish terrorism, both Arabs and British soldiers were under attack by the Hebrew militia that had resolved to occupy Palestine in its entirety by hook or by crook. The rising violence in Palestine finally led to the event called the Nakbah, or in English, the "Catastrophe." This was the first episode in the history of the ethnic cleansing and genocide of native Palestinians by Zionist paramilitary forces (before the birth of Israel) and the IDF (after the establishment of the Zionist state). The event of *al-nakbah* always reminds people that Israel was founded upon the dead bodies of countless civilians, including women and children. The fire that started burning in the heart of every Palestinian boy and girl who lost their parents, siblings, or other family members—the fiery flames of revenge and the desire to take back what's rightfully theirs—is still burning. Even though Israel started Nakbah 2.0 in October by bombing Gaza and massacring Palestinian children, it has once again reminded all peace-loving, colonialism-hating people in the world that no country established upon the corpses of dead children has the right to self-determination.

Sadly, many right-wing extremists and Islamophobes either downplay the brutality of Nakbah or deny that it happened in the first place. Indeed, prominent Zionists have tried to rewrite history dishonestly by claiming that Nakbah happened because Arab leaders simply "asked" Palestinians to leave Palestine and move somewhere else. This blatant example of Nakbah denial stems from the deep-rooted hatred Jews have for gentiles. However, whether Zionists mock the existence of a millennia-old Palestinian identity or deny the truth about the story of the genocide that is the Nakbah. this book will dismantle all these lies. You'll learn what the Nakbah actually was and how it proves the falsehood of Israel's foundational myths.

In simple words, a country like Israel doesn't have any right to defend itself, and the story of the Nakbah proves beyond doubt that organizations like Hamas have every right to defend themselves from the atrocities committed by White squatters from Europe and America.

So, let's start exploring the events leading to the Nakbah in 1948 as briefly as possible.

Long Walk to Bloodbath: Key Events Leading to Nakbah

> "Al-Nakbah is associated with a rapid de-Arabization of the country. This process has included the destruction of Palestinian villages. About 418 villages were erased, and out of twelve Palestinian or mixed towns, a Palestinian population continued to exist in only seven ... Arabic names were replaced by Zionist, Jewish, or European names. This renaming continues to convey to the Palestinians the message that the country has seen only two historical periods which attest to its "true" nature: the ancient Jewish past and the period that began with the creation of Israel." — Ahmad H. Sa'di.

The year was 1948, one of the many years filled with grief and passion for displaced Palestinians, people who were forced to part ways with their ancestral villages to make room for foreigners who claimed these lands in the name of their long-forgotten forefathers from two thousand years ago. The war-torn streets of Jerusalem were screaming in pain as the sun set over the dusty buildings—or what remained of the homes that once stood there. The once-thriving city, now a battleground, was a testament to the devastating consequences of conflict. Born from the ashes of the Holocaust and over the corpses of the innocent children of Palestine, the newly established state of Israel was proclaiming its victory over the deniers of a Jewish state. Little did they realize that they had done to the Palestinians exactly what Nazis did to the Jews during the Holocaust. The victims of one genocide were perpetrating another one against a people who had nothing to do with the Holocaust at all.

A group of Arab refugees, worn and weary, were clinging to the hopes of a better life. Foreigners from Europe and America were on the cusp of usurping their ancestral homelands, and these refugees couldn't do anything about it. Several events transpired between the events of WWII and the establishment of the monstrosity that is the state of Israel, summarized here for brevity:

November 1947: Resolution 181 was passed in the General Assembly, which proposed turning Palestine into two separate states, one for Arabs and the other for Jews, putting Jerusalem under UN administration. But the Arabs rejected this plan as they saw it for what it really was: a sly Jewish strategy to take over half of the Arab ancestral homeland.

Clashing over land ownership issues because a sizable population of Hebrews had colonized the ancestral homeland of native Palestinians. The conflict continued to escalate as British troops prepared to withdraw after plunging the whole region into chaos.

April 1948: The infamous Deir Yassin Massacre took place in which merciless Zionist terrorists slaughtered hundreds of men, women, and children. This event became so famous that it shook Israeli sympathizers abroad, such as Albert Einstein, who famously condemned these acts of terrorism. Sadly, Einstein's words fell on deaf ears, as the Zionist regime was planning to do far worse things to displaced Palestinians.

May 1948: The British Mandate died an unholy death and, like a disgusting entity emerging from the depths of a foul-smelling swamp, out came the State of Israel. Naturally, it triggered the Arab-Israeli War of 1948 (which will be explored in later sections). It's estimated that at least 750,000 Palestinians were driven away from their homelands by Zionists who, it seems, loved to persecute civilians instead of fighting one-on-one with soldiers.

February and July 1949: Armistice agreements finally put an end to the war but couldn't put an end to the ongoing genocide of the natives. Palestinians who were driven away from their homes are still waiting for "permission" to return to their homeland. They recall the events of their banishment as the Nakbah or Catastrophe.

In short, the events of the Nakbah left a deep scar on the collective memory of the Arab world, especially the natives of Palestine. Palestinians, who lost their homeland, watched their families get displaced and their cities decimated by colonizers from Europe, instilling a deep sense of injustice and betrayal. These sentiments continued simmering for generations to come. As the dust settled, the world watched the State of Israel taking its first tentative steps. It was the first post-WWII mega-colonial project in human history. Contrary to Jewish hopes and aspirations, Palestinians weren't going to simply walk away from their ancestral lands; they pledged to fight and resist the Hebrew occupation. The birth of Israel was marked by the promise Arabs had made to the olive trees of Palestine, "We will come back for you; we won't forget you or forgive the ones who took you away from us, O the land of our fathers!"

The Seeds of Chaos: Unearthing the Roots of Arab-Israeli Conflict

> *"To my parents who built their house in Bethany, which is five kilometers outside Jerusalem, the Nakba is as real today as it was 64 years ago. But my parents aren't allowed to live in their house if they want to keep their Jerusalem ID. They must rent an apartment in Jerusalem. Yet the Ma'aleh Adumim settlement is within walking distance from my parent's home in Bethany. It is perfectly "legal" for Israeli Jews to live there, but not for my parents. Every time my father travels through checkpoints to water the garden he planted and to take care of the empty house—while not being allowed to spend a night there—he relives the Nakba again. When my aunt, who was born in Jerusalem but lives in*

Hebron, cannot come and visit us in Jerusalem because she is a "West Banker," we live the Nakba again." — Aziz Abu Sarah.

I once read the famous anti-Zionist Iraqi Jew historian Avi Shlaim, who said: "Antisemitism is a threat created by European Jews for European Jews. And my mother used to talk a great deal about the wonderful Muslim friends that we had in Baghdad. And one day I asked her, 'Did we have any Zionist friends?' and she said, 'No!'" This statement demonstrates that Zionism was an ethno-fascist, Euro-centered movement, an offshoot of the much-hated White supremacy.

Shlaim added: "Zionism is an Ashkenazi thing. It's nothing to do with us. And I think that reflected the predominant view of Iraqi Jews. And looking at it from the other end, the Zionist movement never had any real interest in the Jews of the East. It revolved around the Jews of Europe and establishing a Jewish state in Palestine for European Jews." He wrote extensively about his experiences and views, particularly criticizing Zionism and the state of Israel for their treatment of Jews from Arab countries.

Some people on Twitter quipped that you aren't doing enough about the cause of Palestine if some vile Zionist hasn't labeled you an antisemite yet. Many Zionists, when they don't have any more talking points or frail arguments to defend the bombing of Gaza or the massacre of 17,000 Palestinian children, switch tactics and start accusing that critic of Israel of being a Jew-hater. It becomes even more amusing when some senseless Zionists start accusing countries like Spain and Ireland or even President Joe Biden of working for Hamas. When it comes to this, I'm always reminded of the words of the poet Mahmoud Darwish, who famously said: "*I will continue to humanize even the enemy… The first teacher who taught me Hebrew was a Jew. The first love affair in my life was with a Jewish girl. The first judge who sent me to prison was a Jewish woman. So, from the beginning, I didn't see Jews as devils or angels, but as human beings.*"

Also, keep in mind the very first quotes attributed to a key Hamas spokesperson who said: "*It means that we don't fight Jews because they*

31

are Jews. Our struggle is only against those who occupied our lands." These quotes explain the Arab-Israeli conflict as eloquently as possible. The conflict isn't due to some sort of Jew-hatred Arabs harbor; Palestinians want to dismantle the State of Israel not due to its Jewish roots but because it's a colony of white-skinned foreigners on their ancestral lands. Labeling Palestinian resistance as antisemitism would be akin to calling Nelson Mandela a racist terrorist who merely hated White people for the color of their skin. Or it'd be like accusing Malcolm X of being a vile racist simply because he wanted to stop anti-Black violence with violence. He felt that freedom, justice, and equality should be achieved "by any means necessary."

Just like Malcolm X justified using violent methods to subdue the White oppressors in the US, it's fair for Arabs to fight their Israeli oppressors and forcefully drive them away from Palestine. Now, European or American authors may try to portray the Arab-Israeli conflict as a "complex or multifaceted issue" with roots in the struggle for control over the Holy Land. However, the truth is not complex. In fact, it is extremely straightforward. In the words of Malcolm X, *"The problem that exists in Palestine is not a religious problem ... It is a question of colonialism. It is a question of a people who are being deprived of their homeland."* One may argue that the Israel-Palestine conflict is simply a question of why Arabs should bear the burden of European guilt. Why do Arabs have to pay for the failure of Europeans to protect the Jewry? Why are Arabs being punished for the crimes committed by Germans under the Nazi regime in Europe?

The killing of Hind Rajab wasn't merely a great tragedy but one of many instances in which the IDF brutes opened fire on children—who were fleeing from bombardment and destruction—and then denied they had anything to do with the killing. In January 2024, six-year-old Hind Rajab and her family fled Gaza City only to meet Israeli troops who opened fire and killed Hind's family. The little girl survived, and PRCS paramedics tried to rescue her. Twelve days later, she and her rescuers were found dead. The death of Hind Rajab was important for two reasons:

Adultification: Many media outlets in the UK and the USA described Hind Rajab as if she were an adult killed in the crossfire. They called her "young lady" to try to shift attention away from the fact that Jewish soldiers killed Hind's family while injuring her and later killed her when she was being rescued by the medics (Mahdawi, 2024).

Jewish privilege: The Western media was quick to believe Israeli lies and assumed that there were no Israeli troops present in the vicinity when Hind died. Many Zionist accounts were so shameless that they blamed Hamas fighters for murdering Hind Rajab. It's one of many accounts of Jewish privilege where the heinous crimes committed by Israelis are either sugarcoated or blatantly justified.

Forensic investigation reveals
HIND RAJAB'S car was hit with
355 bullets and finds it "not plausible"
that the Israeli tank couldn't see children
inside the car

However, everything changed in June 2024. A UK-based research group called Forensic Architecture found that an Israeli military vehicle pummeled the Hind family vehicle with 335 bullets and that the Jewish sharpshooters knew they were hitting a child. The investigation also reported that the Israeli tank fired 750 to 900 rounds every minute "positioned within thirteen to twenty-three meters" when it killed Hind's fifteen-year-old cousin. The report concluded by stating: "It's not plausible that the shooter could not have seen that the car was occupied by civilians, including children." (Staff, 2024)

Nevertheless, these conflicts still exist to this day. Whether it's the burning of babies in ovens by Zionists in 1948 (a story the Hasbara propaganda accounts fabricated about the October Seven event) or the killing of Hind Rajab, Arabs are the ones paying the price. They're the ones who lost their lands, their women are imprisoned, their men massacred, their children used for target practice by Zionists, their faith mocked, and their identity denied. And the savage irony is they're the ones accused of being brutish and uncivilized. It's a mirror image of how people of color were the victims of discrimination and lynching by racist Whites of the South. They, too, were described as uncivilized by their very oppressors. Israelis are following in the footsteps of their fascist brothers, Nazis and neo-Nazis.

Gaza remains a focal point of the conflict. The Gaza Strip came under Israel's military control in 1967. Now, even though Israel claims to have freed Gaza, the tiny strip remains blockaded by Zionists from all sides. Also, this region has been the site of several major conflicts, including the 2008-2009 Gaza War and the 2014 Gaza War. The conflict in Gaza has resulted in significant human suffering, with thousands of Palestinians killed and injured and widespread destruction of infrastructure and property.

But no discussion on the ongoing genocide in Gaza can be complete without discussing the famous Arab-Israeli War of 1948. In the next section, we'll historically analyze that war and discuss the Palestinian refugee crisis created during the Nakbah. That context will help you to better understand the plight of the Palestinians.

Arab-Israeli War: War of Independence or Prelude to the Palestinian Holocaust?

A small church sits atop a small hill in northern Galilee, the land where Jesus of Nazareth once roamed with his apostles. Once a point of veneration for many Palestinian Christians, it's now in ruins, one of the last remaining buildings that were a part of the little village of Iqrit. Iqrit was one of many cities that lost their native population and were decimated by the marauding Zionist army in 1948.

The events of the Nakbah and the Arab-Israeli War didn't only affect the Muslims of Palestine but affected the local Christian population as well. Meet Samer Toume, whose grandparents were among the hundreds of Christians the IDF expelled from Iqrit. Iqrit reminds Samer of his roots. Iqrit is one of many towns that were razed to the ground to make way for the creation of the idol of Israel, worshiped by Jews as if it were another golden calf made to dissuade them from venerating the One True God. Around 530 villages were destroyed in the Nakbah event. Samer points out that the Zionists forbade the natives from ever returning to their ancestral lands unless they were dead—then they were allowed to be buried in Iqrit. However, rebuilding their demolished homes or cultivating crops remains illegal. Unfortunately, unlike Samer, many Palestinians can't even bury their dead in their ancestral lands. Entire generations were uprooted when the state of Israel was established, and Arabs were punished by their Zionist oppressors for resisting the occupation. This is the story of the Arab-Israeli War of 1948.

Zionists may try to distort historical truths by calling it the "War of Independence," just like the British maligned the character of Muhammad Mahdi of Sudan by portraying him as a madman. Or, like they portray the Houthis as terrorists even though they're the ones resisting the terrorism committed by Israelis and Americans. Just as the Indian War of Independence (1857) is described as the Sepoy Rebellion by British historians.

As the British were preparing to withdraw from Palestine, tensions escalated between Arabs (who wanted to reclaim their sovereignty and prevent foreigners from taking over their ancestral homeland) and Zionist elements (who wanted to take over someone else's land and create a Jewish nation on the corpses of Palestinian children).On May 14, 1948, as the British Mandate expired, Zionist forces declared the establishment of the State of Israel, triggering the 1948 Arab-Israeli War. Arab forces from Egypt, Transjordan (Jordan), Iraq, Syria, and Lebanon invaded Palestine, with Egyptian forces surrounding the Negev and Arab forces overrunning the Jewish quarter of Jerusalem's Old City.

Zionist and pro-Israel historians may argue that both sides caused the Arab-Israeli War of 1948. A fair observer, however, will realize that the war began when Zionist paramilitary forces started murdering kids in Palestine. The massacres committed by these filthy savages enraged the local Arab populace. They decided to defend their women and children and avenge the deaths of their martyrs. One of the key reasons why Arabs fought Zionists was the Deir Yassin Massacre that took place just a month before the beginning of the Arab-Israeli War. I won't go into the details of this massacre. It is enough to quote the testimony of an eyewitness.

In his book *Palestine Rising*, the author quotes a San Diego-based Palestinian immigrant named Othman Akel, who survived the 1948 massacre with his brother and later escaped to America. Akel said, "I watched my father, my brothers, my sisters, and my grandfather being killed in front of my own eyes. I saw the Zionist terrorist soldiers ordering the bakery man of the village to throw his son in the oven and burn him alive. The son is holding the clothes of his father tightly and crying from fear and pleading with his father not to do it. The father refuses, and then the soldiers hit him in his gut so hard that it caused him to fall on the floor. Other soldiers held the son, Abdel Rauf, threw him in the oven, and told his father to toast him well done. Other soldiers took the baker himself, Hussain al-Shareef, and threw him too in the oven, telling him, 'Follow your son; he needs you there.'"

The war that raged for the next ten months led to thousands of casualties on both sides. But it was a very easy victory for the newly established State of Israel, which had not only state-of-the-art weaponry but also had American support on its side.

This war displaced almost a million Palestinians who had to seek refuge in Gaza, the West Bank, Jordan, and many other places. But it also turned Gaza into a center of Palestinian resistance and a movement that shook the world to its core. The fighting continued until January 1949, when armistice agreements were reached between Israel and each of the Arab states. These agreements fixed a temporary frontier between Israel and its neighbors, with the Green Line becoming the generally recognized boundary between Israel and the West Bank.

Today, the Palestinian refugee crisis has intensified as Israel repeatedly attacks refugee camps and directly targets civilians under the guise that "Hamas uses civilians as human shields." In the next section, we will explore the rabbit hole of the Palestinian diaspora and discuss how the Jews from Europe handed their tragedies to their Palestinian victims and created a cycle of violence. They may have gained a homeland but at what cost? Who suffered so that European Jews could get a haven in the Middle East? The Palestinian refugee crisis is a pertinent example of how post-WWII colonialism hasn't ended but just changes shape. The war against colonialism rages on even today. But this battle requires martyrdom, and Palestinians are offering themselves as martyrs for the sake of resistance against occupation.

Palestinian Refugees: The Aftermaths of the Zionist Occupation

> *"The origin of Israel's contemporary regime over Palestinians is found in the racist ideology of late 19th century European colonialism. This ideology was shared by the dominant stream of the Zionist movement, which was founded in Europe and would later establish the state of Israel." — This is a major theme of the BDS Movement.*

"Palestinians are troublemakers, and that's why they have been expelled from all Arab countries," a Zionist and Israel apologist said on X, formerly Twitter. But then every pro-Palestine activist reminded him that Jews had been expelled from over a hundred countries in the past 2,500-plus years. "Won't you apply the same principles on Jews and call them troublemakers now?" people asked the Zionist. Others reminded him that millions of Palestinian refugees already live in Jordan. In fact, Jordan hosts the largest group of banished Palestinians. Even the Queen of Jordan is a Palestinian by descent. "Jordan has never expelled its Palestinian immigrants. The Black September event involved a tiny group of Palestinians who tried to overthrow the King and were then expelled," an anonymous account explained. "Jordan still hosts over 2 million Palestinians, many of whom have attained Jordanian citizenship."

Maligning Palestinian refugees and portraying them as troublemakers instead of the victims of genocide has always been a key tactic Zionists employ. After all, this technique has been taken directly from the playbook of White supremacists, right-wing extremists, and fascists. These right-wing extremists who are fervent apologists of European colonialism always portray the victimized nations, i.e., Native Americans, Black people, Indians, etc., as the "bad people" who resisted modernization and deserved to be ruled over by the White race. Modern-day Zionists belong to the same category of racists; the only difference is that Zionists use Talmudic ideologies to portray themselves as the "master race" and native Palestinians as gentiles who must choose between exile and servitude under Zionist rule. The Palestinian refugee crisis originated when natives refused to live under Zionist rule as slaves. They were punished with banishment, just as Assyrians and Babylonians banished the Jews of the pre-Christian era.

Today, Israel remains the epicenter of post-WWII European colonialism. Even though Zionist entities try to portray the Israel-Palestine conflict as a religious clash, it's basically an ongoing struggle against the remnants of Western imperialism. It's a battle to reclaim the Palestinian homeland. In the words of Wesam Ahmed, "*The Palestinian struggle is not just a struggle against occupation, apartheid, and colonialism; it is a struggle against imperialism. We need and deserve a new, just, and equitable international order—one that truly upholds the principles of fairness, equality, and respect for the rights of all nations, regardless of their size or geopolitical significance.*" This conflict won't be over until Israel is completely dismantled (just like the apartheid-waging South Africa or the slave-owning America) and Palestinians are allowed to return to their ancestral lands.

After the events of the Nakba, many Palestinians fled to the neighboring countries of Jordan, Lebanon, and Syria, while others sought refuge in the West Bank and Gaza Strip. In Gaza, the influx of Palestinian refugees led to the creation of several refugee camps, including Jabalia and Beach. These camps were established to provide temporary shelter and aid for the displaced Palestinians, but they quickly became permanent fixtures in Gaza's landscape. The camps were overcrowded and lacked basic infrastructure, with many residents living in tents or makeshift shelters.

This refugee crisis significantly impacted the demographic makeup of Gaza. Over 2 million refugees lived in Gaza before Israel committed genocide against them in 2023/2024. These densely populated refugee camps are marked by hunger and poverty. Many Gazans lack basic healthcare and education services. The presence of a large refugee population has also shaped the political and social dynamics of Gaza. Many Palestinians in Gaza identify strongly with their refugee status and the struggle for the right to return to their ancestral homes. Unlike what Zionists lead you to believe, Palestine faced a humanitarian crisis even before the events of October Seven due to what a resolution of the UN General Assembly referred to as an "unholy alliance between Portuguese colonialism, South African racism, Zionism, and Israeli imperialism."

The Israeli blockade, overcrowded refugee camps, and a series of military conflicts (often started by the IDF who are trying to use Palestinian kids for target practice or attack the honor of burqa-clad women) have worsened the situation. Palestinians were already facing a severe shortage of resources and basic services in Gaza. Many refugees in Gaza live in poverty and lack access to adequate food, water, and healthcare. The humanitarian crisis in Gaza has been exacerbated by the COVID-19 pandemic, which placed an additional strain on the already overburdened healthcare system. The pandemic also led to increased unemployment and economic hardship, particularly among the refugee population. Even in the West Bank, people were living under such dire conditions before the events of October 7, 2023, that it was labeled the deadliest year in regional history (For Palestinians in the West Bank, 2023).

Today, over seven decades have passed since Palestinians lost their homes to European robbers and brutal invaders of the United States. The shadow of the Nakbah hasn't passed; instead, the Catastrophe opened a path of justice, struggle, and resistance for Palestinians. Even though Zionists have tried their best to shut down the resistance movement, they have failed miserably. In the words of Ben-Gurion, *"We must do everything to ensure they never do return ... The old will die, and the young will forget."* But the schemes of savage Zionists haven't been successful.

The Path of Struggle after the Nakbah: What's Next?

> *"We need to flatten entire neighborhoods in Gaza. Flatten all of Gaza. The Americans didn't stop with Hiroshima—the Japanese weren't surrendering fast enough, so they hit Nagasaki, too. There should be no electricity in Gaza, no gasoline or moving vehicles, nothing. Then they'd really call for a ceasefire."*
> — Gilad Sharon, the son of Ariel Sharon.

It was a stormy night in June 2024 when Fatimah was sitting outside her tent, eating stale bread, drinking rainwater, and watching evening clouds slowly move across Gaza's skyline. The once-vibrant coastal enclave of Gaza, a symbol of the ongoing Palestinian struggle, was a testament to the devastating consequences of conflict and displacement. For decades, the people of Gaza had endured the pain of exile, their lives forever altered by the events that unfolded in the mid-twentieth century. But then the second Nakbah had made survival even more difficult.

As the shadows lengthened, Fatimah found herself lost in thought, remembering her parents and sisters who all perished when Zionists mercilessly bombed the Rafah refugee camp at the end of May. The little girl had grown up hearing stories of her grandparents' life before the Nakbah, the catastrophic events of 1948 that had torn her people from their homes and scattered them across the region. Her grandparents had fled their village near Yaffa, carrying only the clothes on their backs and the hope of one day returning. Now, she was living in another Nakbah. The dream of returning to her ancestral lands was now a distant memory, overshadowed by the harsh realities of living under genocide. Every day was a struggle. Little Fatimah missed the days when her most pressing issues involved facing bullies at school or not doing so well on her math tests. Now, surviving yet another day was a miracle; she and her relatives—who were decreasing in number day by day—never knew if they would wake up the next morning alive.

Yet, despite the hardships, the people of Gaza clung to their identity, their culture, and their determination to reclaim their rightful place in the land of their ancestors one day. Fatimah has shared the determination of her people. As she watched the sun dip below the horizon, she marveled at the bravery of her nation; Palestinians had never lost hope despite burying their entire families. They fought for their rights, dignity, and freedom using whatever means available to them. Some turned to armed resistance, while others embraced nonviolent protest and civil disobedience. Still, others, like Fatima's parents, chose to focus on building a better life for their children despite the obstacles that stood in their way. "But, in the end, they, too, perished," Fatimah said to herself. "They chose the path of least resistance but met with a terrible end. They decided not to fight back, but nonviolence didn't save them from Israeli atrocities." Like her older brother, who was determined to join Hamas and avenge his dead parents, she, too, believed that peace was never an option.

As the stars began to twinkle in the night sky, Fatima rose from her seat and made her way inside, where the sounds of laughter and conversation filled the air. Everyone was talking about the next steps. "What to do now? How do they survive this genocide and escape the brutalization of their people?" Like all Gazans living in refugee camps, Fatimah and her brother realized that the road to resistance was the only means to gain freedom. Her brother had written this quote by Malcolm X in his diary with an Arabic translation: "*Free-*

dom is never safeguarded peacefully. Anybody who is depriving you of freedom isn't deserving of a peaceful approach by the ones who are deprived of their freedom."

The people of Gaza—and Palestine as a whole—would never give up their fight for a better future, one where they could live in peace and dignity, free from the shadows of the past. It was a struggle that had defined their lives and one that would continue to shape the lives of generations to come. The only way they can preserve their civilization is to fight back.

In the next chapters, we'll discuss the culture of Gaza and its civilization. We'll explore the details of the ongoing Gazan genocide in detail. Keep reading to unveil more truths about the history of Gaza and the struggle of Palestinians for their right to return to the lands where their ancestors' bones lie sleeping.

4. Gaza's Culture and Demographics: Reversing the Effects of the Dehumanization of the Palestinian People

"We [Palestinians] are not sub-humans. Let me repeat: We are not sub-humans. We will never accept a rhetoric that denigrates our humanity and reneges our rights—a rhetoric that ignores the occupation of our land and oppression of our people." — Riyad Mansour, the Palestinian ambassador to the UN.

Many Palestinians have sorrowful stories of how they were expelled from their homes during the events of the al-Nakbah. Here is my own family's story.

My father was born in Palestine in 1918, and my mother in 1922. I only remember my grandmother from when I was three or four, climbing on her back at our two-story house in the village of Bidya not far from Nablus —it's my only memory of her. I knew my grandfather, a tall, serious man with a cane. I once visited the grave of my great-grandfather, Sheikh Ali, a respected religious figure.

He left us over 30 dunums of land, and we still have the original deeds from 1930 and 1961, passed down from my grandfather to my father, and now it is mine and my brothers. I inherited some of that land, including olive trees. These old documents, with signatures and thumbprints for those who couldn't sign, are priceless to me—worth more than the Balfour Declaration mentioned in Chapter 2.

In November 2022, after more than five hours of questioning by a young Israeli customs officer on the borders right out of Jordan, because I said I was visiting my land in Nablus area, I finally reached our land—a place my family has owned for generations and where I was born. Despite this, I was still interrogated upon entering my homeland. This is a photo of my family taken before I was born at the famous Tefaha studio in Nablus. "Tefaha" means "apple," and it was the name of the photographer, which I heard once from my strong, tall mother.

You can see that Palestinians had culture, sophistication, and style. Yes, that's my father, Mohamed Ali Rabi, my mother, Thebe Mousa Taha, and my brother and sister, Ali and Jawidah. While Churchill once said, "History is written by the victors," it doesn't mean that those who didn't win have no history to tell. Their stories are less often told, but they are just as real. That olive tree you see behind me on the back cover, called Olive Romi, has a massive trunk that originates from Rome. We had over 300 of these trees, but we can't harvest even a single olive—just the photograph you're looking at!

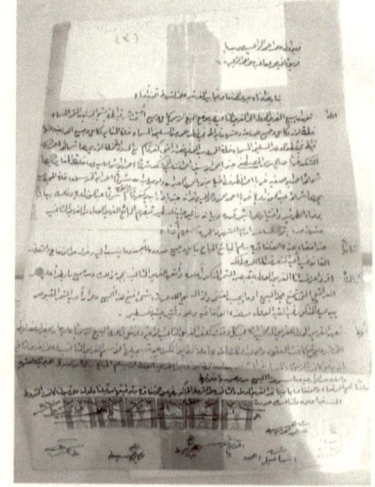

The Dehumanization of Palestinians

The world was shocked in the early days of June when American troops, disguised in an aid truck, came to the shores of Gaza and, along with their counterparts in the IDF, "rescued" four hostages from Hamas's custody. In an attempt to save four Jewish lives, they ended up massacring more than 200 Palestinians. Social media unitarily condemned this botched rescue mission and called it a full-blown massacre. However, the blood-soaked Jewish press had a different opinion.

"It doesn't matter that hundreds of Palestinians died in that operation," chimed in one X (formerly known as Twitter) user. "A single Jewish life is worth 1,000 Palestinian lives. As per this logic, it was *actually* very generous of us to kill so few Palestinians." This blatant example of dehumanizing the men and women of Gaza is not the first example of Israeli fascism. Jewish rabbis have been saying for the past three decades that a million Arabs aren't worth a single Jewish fingernail (Kraft, 2019).

Similar sentiments are being voiced today as Zionists dehumanize Palestinians and then wonder why people compare them to Nazis. When the Borat-fame, Oscar-winning screenwriter Lee Kern calls all Palestinians savages, Visegrad 24 justifies the death of civilians in Gaza, or Seth Crosby describes the ethnic cleansing of Palestinians as "a much-needed cleansing... Israel isn't targeting humans," we realize why there's a need for the world to see Gazans as they *genuinely* are: ordinary people who want to live normal lives in their forefathers' country. However, the genocidal statements out of Israel show that Israeli citizens do not even see their Palestinian neighbors as human beings.

Even in October, when the genocide of the Gazans had just begun, the President of Israel shocked the world by saying this phrase: "There are no innocent civilians in Gaza." (Ghanem, 2024)

The world already knew that Hebrew society was rotten to the core, but it was in October when everyone realized that Israelis had become full-on fascists. After all, Israeli politicians are now welcoming the new tide of right-wing governments being formed in Europe. The world can see that the descendants of the victims of the Holocaust have now become perpetrators of genocide themselves. For a genocide scholar and students of world history, it's not very surprising. There have been instances in the past when the Tutsi minority, which had been the victim of the Rwandan Genocide in 1994 perpetrated by the Hutu majority, returned the "favor" by committing genocide against them a decade later.

"This is a struggle between the children of light and the children of darkness, between humanity and the law of the jungle"
- Benjamin Netanyahu, Prime Minister of Israel

"It's an entire nation out there that is responsible. This rhetoric about civilians unaware is absolutely not true. We will fight and it will break their backbone" - Isaac Herzog, President of Israel

"I have ordered a complete siege on the Gaza Strip. There will be no electricity, no food, no fuel, everything is closed. We are fighting human animals and we are acting accordingly"
- Yoav Gallant, Israeli Defense Minister

"We are now rolling out the Gaza Nakba. Gaza Nakba 2023. That's how it'll end" - Avi Dichter, Israel's Agriculture Minister

"Israel has a very clear message to our enemies. We are saying to them, look what's happening in Gaza – you are going to get the same treatment if you attack us. We are going to wipe you off the face of the Earth" - Nir Barkat, Israel's Minister of Economy

"They can go to Ireland or deserts; the monsters in Gaza should find a solution by themselves. There is no place for the Gaza Strip, there should be no existence for the north of the Gaza Strip"
- Amihai Eliyahu, Israel's Heritage Minister

"An enemy that should be annihilated with all means necessary"
- Benny Gantz, Israeli War Minister

"I welcome the initiative of the voluntary emigration of Gaza Arabs to countries around the world. This is the right humanitarian solution for the residents of Gaza and the entire region after 75 years of refugees, poverty and danger" - Bezalel Smotrich, Israel's Finance Minister

This narrative of dehumanization didn't just start after the events of October Seven; it existed even before October. For example, an Israeli far-right minister took everyone by surprise when he proclaimed in March 2023 that there were no Palestinian people (Gold, 2023). Whether they deny the Nakbah or the nationhood of the Palestinian people, dehumanization has become an integral component of Jewish fascism in Israel and the United States. Whether it's Netanyahu describing the Gaza Genocide, in a now-deleted tweet, as a war between the children of light and the children of darkness or Yoni Leviatan admitting that he doesn't care at all about all the damage and destruction in Gaza, this dehumanization itself is evidence that Palestinian civilians are facing genocide right now. It's even apparent from multiple statements by Israeli officials:

Statements by top Israeli officials have mentally regressed us to the thirties and forties when Nazis used to spread similar propaganda about Jews—imagine the souls of the victims of the Holocaust watching their descendants turn into Nazis (Washington, 2024).

Denying the Humanity of Palestinians: How Are Genocides Justified?

> "From beginning to end, [the preliminary Zionist movement] involved acting as if the Palestinian people not only must not exist but had never existed … The United States and Europe owed reparation to the Jews. And they made a people, about whom the least that could be said is that they had no hand in and were singularly innocent of any holocaust and hadn't even heard of it, pay this reparation." — Gilles Deleuze.

A Hollywood movie, *Good Kill*, illustrated the ethical and moral consequences of using remote-controlled drones to target an assumed target. Should a man be given the power to eliminate a life in a faraway country with the flick of a button? It leads to the "PlayStation mentality," in which humans are reduced to blips on the screen, and all humanity is taken out of the mass massacre. Killing innocent people has been reduced to *bug splats* through aerial bombing and drone strikes. That's what makes genocide easier in the twenty-first century. It was easier for Nazis to use gas chambers to exterminate the Jews because they couldn't face their victims at the precise moment of death; it's easier for Americans and Israelis to kill Palestinians once they're dehumanized, treated as sub-humans who are devoid of any humanity, incapable of culture, and undeserving of sympathy.

The famous genocide scholar Edward Waller believes that in the Rwandan genocide, what frustrated the Hutu murderers most was when their Tutsi victims refused to turn their backs on them and insisted on facing the machete-wielding murderers with ferocity in their eyes. It traumatized the murderers as they would then have to live with these memories, haunted by their crimes forever. However, the genocide we see being perpetrated in Gaza is an anomaly in this regard; it's a unique case where the murderers *are* facing their victims—looking at the blown-up skulls of men and dead bodies of breastfed kids with missing limbs—yet they are celebrating these murders. The false story of Hamas beheading forty Jewish babies made the West tremble in rage, yet the photos of dead Palestinian children seem to have no effect whatsoever on the Western Zionists. The debunked story of Hamas's alleged sexual violence on October Seven was welcomed by the Western world, and the false accounts of Israeli propagandists were given preference over a long history of sexual violence perpetrated by Zionists against Palestinian prisoners (men and women alike) along with the August 2024 tragedy when Israeli soldiers almost started a civil war when they were prevented from raping Palestinian detainees (*The Unravelling*, n.d.).

Then there's Lindsay Graham saying, "Gaza is going to look like Tokyo and Berlin at the end of World War II when this is over. And if it doesn't look that way, Israel made a mistake" (Ishisaka, 2023). It casually reminds us of the blatantly racist past of America, a colony built by settlers and immigrants who overpowered the natives in the end and claimed they had more rights over these lands than the people living there for millennia, where the president could get away with calling Muslim immigrants "a Trojan horse."

Another Israeli minister justifies nuking Gaza and even claims that anyone waving the Palestinian flag doesn't have the right to live on the face of the Earth. Another Zionist monster boasts of waging a Nakbah 2.0 to overshadow the first one (Camut, 2023). Again, we shouldn't forget that it's not the first time Israeli ministers, politicians, and religious figures have justified attacking Palestinian civilians (Krauss, 2023). Even a decade ago, warmongers like Ayelet Shaked (one of the lawmakers in Knesset) called for a "collective punishment" to be inflicted upon Gazans, painting all Palestinians as "enemies" (Abunimah, 2017).

In Nazi Germany, Jews were compared to rats and pests that deserved to be thrown out of Europe (Fatima, 2023).

All of this bears a striking resemblance to the Nazi propaganda Goebbels orchestrated to spread the hatred of Jews among Germans, comparing them with rats. Movies like *The Eternal Jew*, if made in 2024, would earn an Oscar, just as movies like *Borat* are celebrated in Hollywood. In films like *You Don't Mess with the Zohan*, Adam Sandler plays the role of a superhuman Jew, a champion of Israel, while the people of Gaza are shown as hapless idiots who can't even dial a phone number properly. Zionists make these movies to dehumanize Gazans especially and all Arabs in general.

We can see Arsen Ostrovsky sharing a picture in which Palestinians are depicted as cockroaches that must be crushed under IDF boots. The visibility of this tweet was limited when people reminded X (formerly known as Twitter) authorities how Nazis and Hutus depicted their Jewish and Tutsi victims as pigs, cockroaches, vermin, microbes, and countless other labels. This dehumanization doesn't just set the stage for genocide but also justifies it.

When the Defense Minister Yoav Gallant says, "We're fighting against human animals," Israelis cheer and yell with delight. That's because

Gallant provides them justification for killing Arab children. When a group of Jewish schoolchildren in Israel sing this song, it reminds everyone that the Gaza Genocide was in preparation for years before the events of October Seven (Project Decolonise, 2023):

"The entire world hates the Arabs,

And the main thing is to kill them one by one!

With these feet, I stepped on my enemy,

With these teeth, I bit his skin,

With these lips, I sucked his blood,

And I still haven't had enough revenge."

When the death of Palestinian children is turned into a meme by Israeli TikTokers, liked by millions as well as shared by thousands—with Israeli channels on Telegram openly celebrating civilian murders as a victory—it's a sign that the Israeli society doesn't view Gazans as fellow human beings anymore. That is precisely why this chapter is being written, so you can learn what the Zionist media doesn't want you to know and see what the Zionist media doesn't want you to see: the very human faces that are currently being crushed in Gaza.

Let's talk about the people of Gaza. Who are they? What do they do? What are their lives like? What sort of music do they like? What kind of foods do they eat? What's their culture like? Learning about the victims of the Gaza Genocide will help you realize why the world is calling for the dismantling of the state of Israel. Once the mask of dehumanization is removed, you'll see the *real* Gaza.

The People of Gaza: Population Statistics and Demographic Trends

The Gaza Strip is twenty-five miles long and 3.7 to 7.5 miles wide, sharing a 14-km border with Egypt. However, the population of Gaza has grown, almost doubling in size between 2020 and 2023 (The West Bank and Gaza, n.d.). This population growth can be attributed to the high birth rate. On average, a Gazan woman will give birth to 3.9 children on average (Surkes, 2024). This seemingly high birth rate may be a response to the ongoing threat of genocide, coupled with the tragic fact that many mothers in Gaza fear the death of their children at an early age due to the constant, violent conflict and oppression. No parent should have to suffer the grief of burying their child. In Gaza, this is a daily occurrence.

Perhaps the most remarkable feature of Gaza's demographics is the fact that 4 in 10 people living in this small territory are under 15. Moreover, one-half of the population of Gaza is aged below 18 (Amer, 2023), a fact that was highlighted at the beginning of the Gaza Genocide in October 2023. When responding to the Jewish accusations that all Palestinians were somehow responsible for killing Israeli civilians, pro-Palestine activists reminded the world that 50 percent of Gazans were kids. Even in 2021, the median age in Gaza was a youthful 19.5 years. One shouldn't forget another key fact: most Gazans weren't born when the last elections in Gaza were held.

When it comes to population density, Gaza is one of the most crowded places on Earth. It's estimated that 6,100 people lived per square kilometer in Gaza before the genocide started. After all, the geographic area of the entire strip is a meager 365 square kilometers. Imagine it as something akin to an open-air prison, in fact, one would not be wrong to describe it as a concentration camp blockaded by Israel on all sides. On the other hand, a much lower population density can be seen in the West Bank (576 people per square kilometer).

Let's visualize Gazans as a besieged population, living with threats like overcrowding, limited resources, strain on infrastructure, and many other challenges that prevent them from accessing adequate housing, education, healthcare, and job opportunities. The density also makes the region more vulnerable to the impacts of conflict, natural disasters, and public health crises. However, Gazans were attempting to make ends meet and make the best of the situation before October Seven. This is reflected in the fabulous literacy rate of Gaza, considering the kind of persecution they face from their Jewish oppressors. The illiteracy rate in Palestine has declined by over 80 percent in the past two decades. In 2019, more than 97 percent of the people living in Gaza and the West Bank were literate. This astounding fact serves to dismantle Zionist propaganda, which portrays a Gazan civilian as a savage despite Israel's lower literacy rate of 91.75 percent.

The population in Gaza is predominantly Arab. More than 98 percent of Gazans are Muslims, belonging to the Sunni school of thought. They follow the Hanafi jurisprudence, but there's a small number of rising Salafis in Gaza as well. Less than 1 percent of Gazans belong to Christianity or other religions. Another notable demographic feature is the high proportion of refugees in Gaza. Around 1.6 million of the 2.1 million residents of Gaza are registered UN refugees, comprising 78 percent of the total population (Haddad, 2021). Sadly, these statistics do not seem to change due to Israel controlling who and what enters or leaves Gaza at all times.

Lastly, despite their remarkably high literacy rate, Gaza is also marked by a wave of unemployment. The most recent studies show that almost 50 percent of Gazans were unemployed (2020). The unemployment streak hit a massive 80 percent in early June as kids began to scramble to feed families, and mothers started asking the nearest Muslim clerics for a *fatwa* that would permit them to cut their limbs off to feed their kids (Balevic, 2024). This is due to the Israeli blockade, as observed by a UNICEF press release two years ago:

> "Largely due to the blockade, poverty, high unemployment rates, and other factors, nearly 80 percent of Gazans now rely on humanitarian assistance.

More than half of Gaza's just over 2 million people
live in poverty, and nearly 80 percent of the youth
are unemployed." — UNICEF.

Now, we'll explore what life in Gaza was like before the events of October Seven. Was Gaza a territory filled with Hamas operatives and mercenaries, as the Jewish media would like you to believe? Or was it a country of happy people who loved life and wanted to celebrate their homeland? Let's learn more about Gaza's art, food, and music scene.

Gaza's Vibrant Cultural Traditions: Music, Dance, and Festivals

Rich in traditions and a past that stretches back several millennia, the Gaza Strip reflects the history of this region, its heritage, and its resilience. From the melodic sounds of traditional Palestinian music to the many colorful displays of dance rituals, from the aromatic flavors of the local Arab cuisine to the festive aura of the jubilant Palestinian community—Gaza's cultural traditions are a testament to the enduring spirit of the region. In this section, we'll explore a few details on Gazan culture:

- **Music:** The musical heritage of Gaza is deeply rooted in its Arab traditions with diverse styles and melodies. The inns and hotels of Gaza play traditional Arab music and modern Palestinian pop music. The folk music of Gaza includes *mijwiz, shebbabeh, yarghool, rababeh, nay, buzuk, qanun, tabla,* and *oud* (Ibrahim, 2022). But you can also find guitars sold in Gazan shops, where you can purchase drums, lutes, and flutes (Almeghari, n.d.). Amal Murkus, DJ Khaled, Mohammed Assaf, and many other musicians of Palestinian descent have used big platforms to showcase the diversity of the cultural identity of Gaza.

- **Dance:** The traditional dance routines of Gaza have various forms. For instance, Dabke is a very famous conventional Palestinian dance performed at weddings (Catherine Vargas Films, 2022). The dance is characterized by its energetic movements, intricate footwork, and lively music. However, this Levantine folk dance is a small example of how dance is deeply rooted in Palestinian identity. The Hawiyya Dance Company and Alrowwad Center are institutions that preserve the dance culture of ancient Gaza. Dancers from Palestine include Assel Qupty, Farah Saleh, Ahmed Alghariz, Hadi Nahleh, to name a few.

- **Festivals:** As Muslims around the world celebrated Eid in April, a celebration of the much-anticipated, blessed month of Ramadan and its successful culmination, Israel bombed Gaza (Afp, 2024). But Gazans have never let anyone forget that festivals are a vital part of their cultural calendar. A festival allows Gazans to come together and celebrate life. Some major festivals held in Gaza and the West Bank include the Grape Festival, the Olive Harvest Festival, Birzeit Heritage Week, the Theater of the Oppressed, the Ramallah Contemporary Dance Festival, and the Artas Lettuce Festival.

A Glimpse into Palestinian Foods: A Nation of Food Lovers

Spicy with lots of pepper—that's how one would describe Gazan cuisine (Bauck, 2023). The local foods of Gaza today are inspired by Mediterranean and Middle Eastern flavors. Many popular dishes like falafel, hummus, and the more famous *shawarma* make Gaza a hub of foodies. Gazans also create sweet pastries like baklava or *ma'amoul*. Many underprivileged Gazans like to eat *mudammas*, a dish made of fava beans. But the best food in Gaza would be something like *maqloubeh* (molded pilafs with rice and veggies) or *mashi* (stuffed courgettes and eggplants).

Besides *maqloubeh*, another dish served on special occasions as a staple of Gaza's culinary heritage is the famous *musakhan*, a dish made with roasted chicken and onions. It also includes sumac, which is loved by every Gazan, young or old. These dishes are not only delicious but also hold significant cultural and historical importance, reflecting the region's history and traditions. However, traditional cuisine's direct competitor is street food. Let's explain how falafel and *shawarma* are made:

- **Falafel:** It's made with crispy chickpeas and spices, often served in a pita with a finely-chopped, tasty salad and tahini sauce.

- **Shawarma:** It's a kind of sandwich made with thinly sliced meat and served in a pita with tahini sauce (yet again) and salad.

But that's not the only great thing about Gazan cuisine. These foods use very diverse ingredients, such as the following:

- Garlic
- Olive oil
- Lemon juice
- Tomatoes and cucumbers
- Eggplants
- Spices like cumin, sumac, and chili
- Herbs like mint, dill, and coriander
- Meat from lambs and goats

Despite all the challenges we've outlined, Gaza's cultural traditions are thriving. The artists, musicians, dancers, and other performers continue to showcase their talents and resilience in the face of oppression. They have found many innovative ways to preserve their cultural heritage. The cultural traditions of the Gaza Strip help these oppressed yet determined individuals keep their sense of identity and belonging alive. That's why we will discuss the cultural heritage of Gaza in the next section. Many Zionists who deny the nationhood of the people of Palestine claim that Palestinians lack an identity of their own and are a "made-up" people. You'll soon learn why this is a bald-faced lie. Let's explore the evidence of the existence of a Palestinian culture and civilization, a truth often denied by Zionist propagandists.

Gaza's Cultural Heritage: War on the Palestinian Civilization

"Libraries serve as cultural repositories, and attacking them is an attack on cultural heritage. What is happening now is a war crime. It goes against the first Hague convention... Israel is trying to erase the connection of the people with their land. It's very clear and intentional. Gaza's heritage is part of its people, its history and their connection." — Isber Sabrine, Syrian archeologist.

In April 2024, UNESCO confirmed that more than forty heritage sites in Gaza were destroyed when the IDF bombed this tiny strip of land (Museums Association, 2024). Israel is busy systematically destroying Gaza's heritage in a disgusting and futile attempt to erase the Palestinians' past. These heritage sites include the prestigious Omari Mosque in Gaza City. The marble columns and towering minarets of this site were severely damaged. Similarly, the Church of St. Porphyrius, considered the third oldest church in the world, was destroyed when an Israeli airstrike targeted the people hiding inside its complex. Blakhiyya served as Gaza's port from 800 BCE to 1100 CE; the Israeli army bulldozed and bombed it. "Archaeological objects from this site were among some 4,000 artifacts in a warehouse that Israeli soldiers have seized," archeologists told the media. Other cultural sites under threat from Israeli bombardment include:

- **Tell Umm Amer:** A monastery where the fourth-century monk Hilarion was born, spanning twenty-five acres in southern Gaza.

- **Qalaat Barquq:** A Mamluk-era fort in Khan Younis, constructed in the late fourteenth century.

- **Qasr el-Basha:** Located in the Old City, this thirteenth-century palace was erected by Baybars when he was visiting Gaza and decided to marry a local woman.

It's argued that 300 to 400 heritage sites are located within this tiny strip. Attacking these sites isn't only a violation of several international laws but also an attempt to destroy the Palestinian civilization as well as the remnants of Gaza's glory. These historic buildings are not physical structures but embodiments of the collective identity and history of the Palestinian people in Gaza, reminding us of the time when Gaza was the epicenter of Mediterranean maritime trade. These mosques, forts, monasteries, palaces, and cemeteries serve as key, tangible symbols that preserve the memories and experiences of generations.

Even the museums in Gaza weren't spared the brutality of Israelis. The Rafah Museum (which housed an ancient collection of coins, copper plates, jewelry, etc.) was bombed in the early days of the Gaza Genocide. Also, the famous al-Qarara Cultural Museum which housed a pottery collection from the Byzantine era sustained substantial damage as a result of Israeli airstrikes. This targeting of cultural sites is part of a broader effort to undermine the Palestinian identity and erase their history. The destruction of their cultural heritage is a profound blow to Palestinians' collective memory and sense of belonging.

However, Palestinians aren't sitting silent; they are resisting, not merely through armed resistance as well as a civil rights movement of their own, but also via art, poetry, and literature. In a small subsection, we'll discuss how Palestinians are writing about their persecution, ensuring that their trials and tribulations are recorded in words that will be read for generations.

Resilience through Art, Literature, and Poetry

"At the cliff of death,
I see myself suspended by a noose,
swaying gracefully with the wind.
I am as free as a firefly glowing in a cave,
a smile on my azure face.
My hands are released,
like an ancient oak tree,
dancing a tango with the breeze."
Written by Haya Abu Nasser (Abraham, 2024)

This Banksy mural appeared in Bethlehem.

Many Palestinian authors and poets have died in the Gaza Genocide. But Gazans haven't stopped talking about their struggle, showing resilience in the face of oppression throughout this conflict. Here are some examples of Palestinian resilience in literary format (*These Are the Poets*, 2024):

- Poetry and literature: Gazan writers have used poetry and prose as media to express their suffering. These literary geniuses have explored the themes of love and resistance in their work as an attempt to show the entire world how it watched Palestine burn and did nothing to prevent the loss of lives in Gaza. These poems show how Gazans stood resilient and determined in the face of adversity. One example is Rafeef Ziadah, whose work was featured in Stories from Palestine.

- Visual arts: Just like Banksy, Gazans have also painted murals and pictures depicting their loss. For example, A'ed Abu Amro was captured by a Turkish journalist Mustafa Hassouna in October 2018. In this picture, Aed clutches a Palestinian flag with one hand while using the other hand to swing a slingshot over his head. In the past, many emerging artistic groups provided young artists a platform for self-expression. Shababeek and the famous Eltiqa Group for Contemporary Arts served as two major institutions.

- Storytelling: Storytelling elements helped many Palestinians send their message across the airwaves. The stories of authors like Areej al-Madhoun provide a glimpse into the daily lives of Gazans but also offer a deeper understanding of their experiences. But storytelling doesn't always have to be in a written format; Palestinian social media activists like Plestia Alaqad document daily life in Gaza amidst the ongoing genocide. Her TikTok videos have become so famous that people started to call her the "Anne Frank of Palestine" (Anabel, 2023). These stories will continue to serve as a symbol of Gazan's resilience and how they resisted the Zionist onslaught with pen, paper, and sword.

Sadly, however, the ongoing conflict in Gaza has had a devastating impact on the region's art and cultural institutions. Many institutions, like Eltiqa and Shababeek, were destroyed or damaged, leaving artists without a platform for self-expression. The war has disrupted access to materials and resources, making it difficult for artists to continue their work. But they have not accepted defeat. Palestinians are refusing to either bow down or leave their homeland. Many stories of heroism and justice are coming from Gaza. In the next chapter, we'll discuss some of these stories.

For now, let's end this chapter with this powerful poem by the martyr Refaat Alareer:

If I must die,

you must live

to tell my story

to sell my things

to buy a piece of cloth

and some strings,

(make it white with a long tail)

so that a child, somewhere in Gaza

while looking heaven in the eye

awaiting his dad, who left in a blaze —

and bid no one farewell

not even to his flesh

not even to himself —

sees the kite, my kite you made, flying up above,

and thinks for a moment an angel is there

bringing back love.

If I must die

let it bring hope,

let it be a story.

The Story of Salha Hamdeen

Salha Hamdeen is a Bedouin girl from Palestine whose story competed with 1,200 works from around the world and won the Hans Christian International Prize for Fiction for her story *Hantoush*. This is what she has to say:

My name is Salha, and I am from the Arab Jahalin School. I live in a small tent in Wadi Abu Hindi. I am 14 years old. In the daytime I study at the reed school, and they made it out of reeds because the soldiers declared our land a closed military zone, where they practice shooting in the farming area. Seventy sheep live with us in the tent, and I milk them after I come back from school, make cheese and sell it to the people of the city. The road here is bumpy because the soldiers prevent us from paving the road, they practice shooting at night, and I hate the sound of gunfire, I almost go crazy from it, so l run, yes I run.

I don't have a bike, because the road is bumpy. I don't have a car or a plane, but I have something to use to escape. Get closer, get closer, I'll confuse you secretly, I have a flying sheep named "Hantoush," black in color and long ears, with two secret wings that he hides inside the wool, and takes them out when I whisper in his ears, O Hantoush, O sheep, I take your wings out from under the wool and sing in his ears, while the soldiers begin to practice shooting, and I ride him and fly, and yesterday we fled to Barcelona. We will tell you something, in Wadi Abu Hindi there are no playgrounds

In (Barcelona) we met "Messi" with big goals, we played with him for long hours, sheep "Hantoush" was standing goalkeeper, and I attacked "Messi" and his team, we scored five goals. Messi wanted to include me and Hantoush to the team (Barcelona) but we refused. We want to return to (Abu Hindi) because the sheep there are waiting for me to not let anyone else milk, my father has been in prison for six years and has nineteen years left. I will tell you a secret: Messi told me that he will visit Wadi Abu Hindi in two years. We will hold the 2018 World Cup in Wadi Abu Hindi, together we will clean the ground of mines, we will build the largest stadium in the world, we will call it "Hantoush Stadium," and the sheep will be the emblem of the World Cup. Welcome to Wadi Abu Hindi! We are all waiting for you.

5. Heroism in Gaza and the Struggle for Justice

> *"I left Gaza yesterday. My heart and my soul are still there, with my patients. I remember their names and their wounds. I will fight until they receive the treatment they need and the justice they deserve. My heart is broken in ways I never knew was possible."* — Dr. Ghassan Abu Sitta.

"Keep thinking of the doctors at Al Shifa who were executed after refusing to abandon their patients." This tweet was posted by Moira Donegan on April 23, 2024. This X user remembers the health workers who sacrificed their lives and didn't abandon their post despite knowing that Israel was incessantly bombing civilian institutions because they could not even entertain the thought of letting their patients die alone. They were not able to move these patients elsewhere. So, they chose to die a hero's death. In the first forty days of the Gaza Genocide, Israel managed to kill more than 200 health workers (Romo, 2023). The present narrative is incomplete without acknowledging these heroes.

Stories of Everyday Heroes in Gaza: Activists, Educators, Healthcare Workers

> *"The scale of the crisis is too great. No health system in the world has the capacity to cope with such bloodshed. The humanitarian response in Gaza today is, therefore, an illusion. We cannot reach our*

patients without being attacked. In Gaza, humanitarians are not heroes, but victims." — Marie-Aure Perreault Revial, Emergency Coordinator for Doctors Without Borders.

I'd like to briefly mention the names of some of the bravest sons of the soil from Gaza. These outstanding and martyrdom-oriented individuals have served valiantly in the past few months. Reading the stories of their bravery will give us all strength and courage.

1. **Rami Abu Shabaan:** This fifty-two-year-old man from the Netherlands had a master's degree in biochemistry. He was killed by Israeli tanks when he was trying to rescue his injured neighbors in Gaza City.

2. **Mohammad Refaat al-Saloul:** He was in his early thirties when he risked his life trying to save a child. As he carried the child back to safety, a rocket fired by the IDF buried him under the rubble along with the child. Refaat didn't just dig himself out; he found the child and saved his life a second time.

3. **Ahmad Abu Khdeir:** This paramedic saved a family when the Israeli army was shelling their town. He knew that the town could be targeted again, but he fearlessly continued searching for wounded civilians so that he could save more lives.

4. **Ahmed Mofeed Mokhalati:** This brave doctor returned from his home in Ireland to help people in Gaza at the Al Shifa Hospital. He slept for just three hours a night while treating patients suffering from head trauma, burns, and internal injuries. Even though the hospital could accommodate only 600 patients, it received 500 to 1,000 patients daily.

Meeting Wael Dahdouh of Al Jazeera after his move to Qatar was a profound honor. Our conversation about the daily struggles and extraordinary heroism of Gazans left a lasting impression, reflecting his unwavering bravery and dedication.

Wael al-Dahdouh: The bureau chief of Al Jazeera learned on the news that an Israeli air strike in the early days of November 2023 had killed his wife, children, and grandchild (Armstrong, 2023). He was on air when he learned about the loss of his family, who were sheltering in the Nuseirat Camp. But Wael acted like a professional, remaining calm while continuing to report the news.

1. **Sobhi Abu al-Hussein:** This brave man turned his fleet of four taxis into rescue vehicles to transport patients from ruined buildings to hospitals. He received frantic calls from a group of survivors who needed rescued immediately. Naturally, Sobhi did that free of charge.

2. **Ghassan Abu-Sittah:** This London-based plastic surgeon returned to Gaza to treat patients. He is a shining example of determination, fortitude, bravery, and self-sacrifice. His uncle, Salman, is a researcher, one of those Palestinians who faced expulsion during the *Nakbah*.

3. **Noor Harazeen:** This thirty-three-year-old reporter fled to southern Gaza after Israel attacked the north. Raised in Dubai, she returned to Gaza in 2006 to serve her homeland. She says, "The biggest challenge as a Gazan journalist is to stay calm and try to hold back my tears." Noor is one of the most important witnesses of Israeli forces killing Palestinian children (Report, 2023).

4. **Yara Eid:** This UK-based Palestinian journalist is only twenty-three years old, yet she's seen a massacre that would shake even a WWII veteran. She talks about how she lost fourteen family members in an Israeli airstrike. However, she continues to do her job, documenting the evidence of Israeli oppression. Even though she currently lives in the UK, the haunting memories of her rela-

tives dying in Gaza keep her awake at night. That's why she continues to speak out about the Gaza Genocide.

5. **Hammam Alloh:** "You think I went to medical school and got my postgraduate degrees for fourteen years so I think only about my life and not my patients?" This was Alloh's answer when asked why he hadn't left his patients at Al Shifa Hospital despite the IDF's intention to hit the facility. As the only nephrologist left in Gaza at one time, this thirty-six-year-old doctor didn't leave his patients alone until he was killed in an Israeli airstrike in November 2023.

In the words of Ghada Ageel, "Palestinian doctors are our heroes, symbols of strength, poise, and hope. At a time when the world has abandoned Gaza and the Palestinians, they have done the opposite. In their words and through their actions, Gaza's doctors are teaching us never to forget and, more importantly, never to give up. Let their colleagues around the world answer this call for justice." We should all salute these heroes who are facing genocide but not giving up on the Palestinian dream (Ageel, 2023).

Political Activism and Resistance Movements in Gaza

> *"Israeli authorities launched "Operation Law and Order," primarily targeting Palestinian protesters. Israeli media said the operation aimed to "settle scores" with those involved and to "deter" further demonstrations ... Most Palestinians arrested were detained for offenses such as "insulting or assaulting a police officer" or "taking part in an illegal gathering" rather than for violent attacks on people or property, according to the Follow-Up Committee for Arab Citizens of Israel." — Press Release by Amnesty International.*

- **March 2018:** Israeli army kills Palestinians in Gaza for protesting (Lee et al., 2018)

- **May 2019:** Sixteen protestors died at the hands of Israeli forces (Holmes & Balousha, 2019)

- **September 2023:** Young protestor Yousef Salem Yousef Radwan was killed for the "crime" of protesting (PressTV, 2023)

Many Zionists on social media argue that Palestinians have never tried peaceful methods to gain freedom. This argument comes from a place of deep ignorance. Just read the above three headlines—the first one is over five years earlier, and the third one is just a month before October Seven—and see. How can Palestinians protest peacefully when demonstrating against Zionist atrocities is a crime in Israel? Many Palestinians (who may or may not agree with Hamas) have attempted to engage in peaceful and mostly nonviolent ways to demand Palestinian statehood (even though Netanyahu has made sure that no Palestinian state would be formed as long as he's in power). Political activism and resistance movements in Gaza have been a crucial aspect of the conflict; various groups and individuals are engaging in protests, boycotts, and other forms of resistance to challenge the Israeli occupation and blockade.

- **The Islamic Resistance Movement:** The movement known as Hamas emerged during the early days of the *Intifada*, or the uprising, of Palestinians. First, it appeared in Gaza and then spread to the West Bank. The militants of Hamas trace their history back to the Muslim Brotherhood (*al-Ikhwan al-Muslimun*). The most successful effort of the Muslim Brothers was the mobilization of hundreds, perhaps thousands, of youths to join Islamist student and youth groups. This drive coincided with the rise and proliferation of mass organizations affiliated with the national movement, particularly student blocs at schools, two-year colleges, and universities.

- **The Great March of Return:** In March 2018, Palestinians who wanted to come back to their forefathers' land decided to demonstrate peacefully. However, Israeli forces answered these demonstrators with violence and oppression. But Palestinians, despite being targeted by Israeli forces, have never backed down. Authorities state that the IDF is responsible for killing more than 250 protestors and injuring more than 30,000 in a single year (Fayyad, 2019).

- **Social media activism:** Additionally, many Palestinians use social media to discuss their aspirations, reversing the effects of the well-funded Israeli media. Thirty-four U.S. states have banned TikTok on government devices. The platform facing potential nationwide bans, allegedly because it became a space where overwhelming evidence of Zionist crimes and Gaza's brutalities. Social media has now become a powerful tool for change, a clear and present reminder to the world that Palestinian lives matter just as much as Israeli lives do. Social media activism for the liberation of Palestine has taken many forms and involves not just Gazans but people from other parts of the world, too. From the grand scale of Mandela to the Instagram account of Alana Hadid or the grassroots activism of Wayne Campbell, all are activists—whether they are social media warriors today or protest leaders tomorrow.

Here are some names and their stories that will help you answer the question "When have Palestinians tried to get their freedom peacefully?" These names belong to activists, orators, and journalists—merely three out of countless demonstrators who tried to reason with Zionists:

- **Abdallah Aljamal:** The world was surprised to learn that the IDF had shot journalist Aljamal over the unproven and utterly baseless accusation of keeping Jewish hostages in his house (Vincent, 2024). A Gaza-based journalist known for reporting Israeli crimes was illegally executed over these fake charges. He protested against the inhumane treatment of Palestinian prisoners in Israeli jails and covered the *March of Return*.

- **Ahed Tamimi:** This brave woman in her early twenties is a prime example of how Gaza's youth have tried to demand their freedom peacefully yet faced persecution. She wrote a memoir about her experiences in *They Called Me a Lioness*. Tamimi gained international fame when she was detained for slapping an Israeli soldier. When she was released from temporary detainment in November, Ahed revealed how Palestinian female prisoners in Israeli camps are treated inhumanely, left with no food or water.

- **Bassem Tamimi:** In early June 2024, Israeli authorities released one of the humblest and most decent protestors, Bassem Tamimi (Agencies, 2023). Often called the "Palestinian Gandhi," this man is a key example of how nonviolent protests are met with forceful suppression in Israel. Tamimi remained in Israel in administrative detention for eight months before being released. Social media users were sad to see the picture of a frail Bassem compared to pictures from the past. They noted how Israeli authorities persecuted their prisoners and treated them the same way that Nazis treated Jewish prisoners in the thirties and forties. Of course, Bassem Tamimi is also the father of the above-mentioned Ahed Tamimi.

But Palestinians aren't the only ones who have spoken up about the plight of Gaza. Many non-Palestinian activists are also part of a global movement of solidarity and support for Palestine's freedom.

International Solidarity and Support for Palestinian Rights

It was a typical day outside the Israeli embassy in Washington DC, as cars moved by and pedestrians strolled casually outside the walled gates of the building. The clock struck 12:58 when a young man, who couldn't have been more than twenty-five years old, walked outside dressed in military fatigues and holding a small camcorder. He had just created a Twitch account and was going to live-stream an extreme act of protest in front of the embassy. Aaron Bushnell planned to self-immolate in protest against the US government's complicity in the Gaza Genocide. Bushnell became one of the rare examples in human history where a person has committed self-burning to protest an act of injustice.

Zionists mocked Aaron's death, stating his act would be soon forgotten. I am mentioning him here to ensure we never forget.

Aaron Bushnell isn't the only person who has demonstrated solidarity and support for Palestinian rights. This movement has been growing since the 2000s. A long list of individuals— activists, politicians, and social media influencers—comes to mind regarding the pro-Palestine movement. From President Jimmy Carter and Norman Finkelstein to army personnel like Bushnell and the Columbia University protestors—these individuals have been critical of Israel's policies and actions in the Palestinian territories, particularly the blockade of Gaza and the construction of settlements in the West Bank. There have been street protests, boycotts, and cultural events to recognize Gaza's plight. Let's discuss some of these examples here.

- **International Solidarity Movement:** Called the ISM, this movement believes in using peaceful, nonviolent methods to bring attention to the Israeli-Palestinian conflict. This organization calls on civilians from all over the world to protest the presence of the IDF in the West Bank and Gaza Strip.

- **Global Solidarity Movement:** This movement draws on historical contexts to advocate for Gaza. They demand the world to recognize the self-determination of the Palestinian people. The success of their efforts lies in policy formulation. They also need to maintain a balanced and constructive approach that appeals to a broad base of support and aligns with international law and principles of human rights.

- **Activists from the world:** Many activists have spoken up about the plight of Gaza. These genius people include Adam Shapiro, the co-founder of the ISM; Huwaida Arraf, another co-founder of the ISM who also remains involved in the Boycott, Divestment, and Sanctions (BDS) Movement; George N. Rishmawi, who also co-founded the ISM and engages in movements like the BDS; and Osama Qashoo, another co-founder of the ISM, filmmaker, activist and artist. Similarly, Tania Bruguera is a Cuban artist who speaks out about the plight of the people of Gaza.

Finally, in 2024, the international tide is turning against the Zionist regime. Things are changing, and more people are speaking up about the plight of Palestinians—their right to embrace statehood is gaining recognition worldwide. Even though Palestine hasn't received UN membership, the goal is in sight. In May 2024, the General Assembly passed a resolution that recognized the rights and privileges of the state of Palestine, deeming it qualified to join the UN as its 194th member. One hundred and forty-three UN members supported the resolution, nine voted against it, and twenty-five abstained (Taheri, 2024).

The UN's approval indicates that Palestinians and their freedom movement have overwhelming support around the globe. Among the 177 countries participating, over 80 percent supported the resolution. Among the ten most populous countries in the world, nine favored the resolution. This signifies that more than one-half of the world's population is on the side of the Palestinians.

By now, you have learned about some of the individuals have spoken up about the Israel-Palestine conflict. Now, we'll discuss the political side of the issue, exploring the key role played by Hamas in Gaza. You will learn how the Gaza Strip is politically structured, who has been ruling it since 1967, and how Israel ensures that Gaza never becomes *truly* independent.

6. Political Situation and Challenges in Gaza

"German reporters harshly asked (me) why I recognize and am friends with Hamas, but my answer was simple: Did the Palestine-Israel conflict start on October 7? No, it began in 1948 when a large number of Palestinians were expelled and killed. Since then, we have witnessed the same genocidal news every single year. Think about Vietnam, Algeria, Indonesia, and South Africa. All their freedom fighters fought for their independence, and are they terrorists? Only colonizers will label freedom fighters as such." — Malaysian Prime Minister Anwar Ibrahim.

It was in April, right after Eid al-Fitr, when the world was shocked to learn that an airstrike had killed the sons and grandchildren of Hamas leader Ismail Haniyeh (Ott, 2024). Haniyeh's grandchildren were targeted because of their relationship with one of the top leaders of Hamas. People began asking: *Who are Hamas's leaders? Where do they come from?* Pictures soon appeared on social media in which Haniyeh was seen, clothed in his usual apparel that made him look like a typical office manager, consoling an old woman, his facial expression betraying a small hint of repressed rage. The Zionist media started asking: *Why doesn't he look sad? Why isn't he crying? Why does he look so composed even after learning that his sons and grandkids have been killed?* Pro-Palestine activists were quick to remind Zionists that it was not the first time Haniyeh had been in this situation; most Hamas leaders have lived with death and horror and suffered terrible losses when they were young. They don't have time to grieve now; their only goal is to avenge the martyrs of Israeli oppression and win the freedom of Palestine.

In this chapter, we'll discuss the political structure of Hamas. You'll learn what Hamas leadership is like, who their rivals are in the struggle for liberation, what sort of support Hamas enjoys in Palestine, and how Hamas ran Gaza before the IDF ousted them after the events of October Seven. The political landscape in Gaza is very complex, mainly due to the IDF blocking this tiny strip of land from all sides. Even though Hamas has been in power since 2007, it could do little due to Israel's refusal to allow Gaza to be independent, citing security concerns as justification for this oppression and the crippling blockade. This blockade led to a severe humanitarian crisis in Gaza, and the locals were suffering major economic hardships even before the genocide. The ongoing conflict has resulted in multiple wars between Israel and Hamas, costing a significant human toll and obliterating infrastructure. The political challenges in Gaza are multifaceted, involving issues such as the blockade, the status of the Palestinian Authority, and the role of regional powers like Iran and Egypt.

Gaza's Political Structure: A Brief Overview

Let's briefly discuss Gazan politics to give you a rough idea of what life is like for Gazans and who their political leaders are. The most recent elections in Gaza took place almost twenty years ago in 2005 when Hamas appeared as the clear winner in these elections with 75 out of 118 seats. Fatah, on the other hand, only managed to win twenty-six seats. One should not forget that these elections were held in ten districts of Gaza; however, major population centers like Gaza City, Rafah, and Khan Younis didn't participate in voting, and many of those who did vote are no longer alive.

However, one mustn't think that Gazans condemn Hamas. Unlike Israel, the US, and a few other countries, the militant organization of Hamas isn't deemed a terrorist organization by the rest of the world. In fact, some of the most recent polls show that most countries don't consider Hamas militants to be terrorists. It's vital to note that the same regimes that describe Hamas as a terrorist group labeled Nelson Mandela an irredeemable terrorist. Hamas enjoys immense support in both West Bank and Gaza. In December 2023, a whopping 42-44 percent of the residents of Gaza and the West Bank supported Hamas (Laub, 2023). As per recent polls and surveys, 40 percent of Palestinians were Hamas supporters (Sawafta, 2024). These surveys cement the status of Hamas as an organization of freedom fighters who believe that armed resistance is the only way to secure a Palestinian state. This is also the major point of contention between Hamas and Fatah.

Hamas and Gaza's Legislative History

In January 2006, legislative elections were held in Gaza, and both Hamas and Fatah secured between 40 percent and 45 percent of the total vote. However, Hamas won 74 out of 132 seats, while Fatah could barely secure 45 seats. After defeating Fatah in the Battle of Gaza (2007)—which we will address in a section—Hamas became the *de facto* ruling party in Gaza and the West Bank. Ismail Haniyeh served as the Gaza and the West Bank Prime Minister from 2007 to 2017 until Yahya Sinwar took over. (AJLabs, 2024)

As you can see from the map on the next page, Gaza has five governorates serving as the administrative districts of this tiny strip of land. Until now, there have been three *de facto* Hamas governments in Gaza (2007, 2012, and 2016). Allegations of corruption and mismanagement have been directed at Hamas. However, investigating these accusations is not the purpose of this book.

Hamas-Fatah Dynamics and Governance in Gaza

The rivalry between Hamas and Fatah is primarily about how to approach

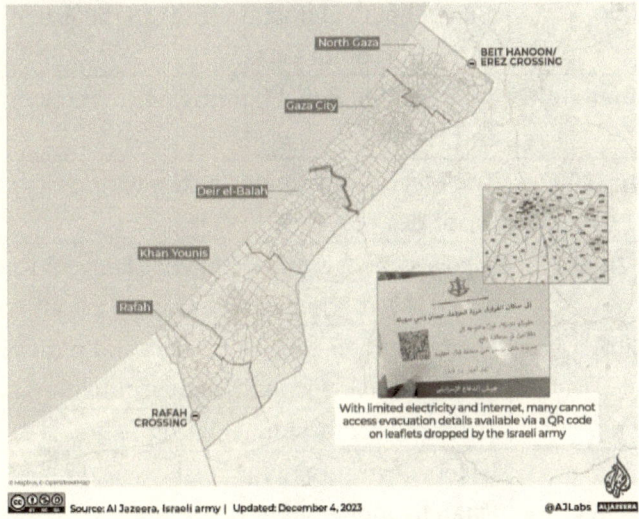

ISRAEL-GAZA WAR

Gaza - nowhere safe to go

After ordering 1.1 million people to leave the northern Gaza Strip, the Israeli army published a map online that divides the besieged enclave into more than 600 numbered zones with instructions to evacuate part of the south.

With limited electricity and internet, many cannot access evacuation details available via a QR code on leaflets dropped by the Israeli army

Source: Al Jazeera, Israeli army | Updated: December 4, 2023   @AJLabs

the issue of the freedom of their motherland. Fatah believes in negotiating the freedom of Palestine with Israel in hopes of bringing about their motherland's independence one day. However, Hamas believes that an armed struggle is the only way to ensure the liberation of their ancestral home. Furthermore, Hamas soldiers don't even recognize the existence of Israel. They treat the Israelis as a band of robbers, a group of squatters.

Now you understand why I believe that Hamas soldiers are freedom fighters. Palestinians support Hamas because seven out of ten Palestinian citizens believe that an armed struggle against Israel is the only way to win their freedom (Tass, 2023).

The history of Hamas shows that they created a government without Fatah's participation, and the subsequent Civil War caused a rift between these organizations. Fatah held its stronghold in the West Bank as a government based in Ramallah, while Hamas held strong in the Gaza Strip. Historians argue that this rift was caused by the death of Arafat (November 2004) and Abbas's lack of charisma. A timeline of the Hamas-Fatah rift looks like this:

January 2006	Hamas wins the polls, deepening the rift with Fatah.
March 2006	Hamas members create a government without Fatah's participation.
June 2006	Gilad Shalit's abduction leads to the intensification of the boycott of Gaza.
December 2006	Sporadic fractional fighting ensues between Fatah and Hamas.
February 2007	The Mecca Agreements puts a temporary stop to hostilities.
March 2007	A government is formed under Haniyeh's leadership, which is comprised of Hamas and Fatah members.
June 2007	Hamas fighters took over Gaza and removed all Fatah members from the government.
2008	Hamas boycotts reconciliation talks.
2009	Israel's Operation Cast Lead catalyzes Hamas and Fatah to cooperate.
May 2011	A unity deal between the two organizations ends the feud (for now).

Israeli blockade and Occupation: Impact on Daily Life and Infrastructure

The government of Israel claims that they left Gaza in 2007. However, the current blockade has trapped Palestinians in this tiny territory, preventing them from experiencing true freedom. This blockade is a major reason why Gaza is politically mismanaged and often lacking basic necessities. The oppressive Zionist regime severely restricts the movement of people and goods. The blockade effectively created a protracted humanitarian crisis, with severe consequences for the well-being and dignity of the population.

How does the Blockade People's Daily Lives?

- **Food insecurity:** Even though Gaza receives aid and food assistance, famine is still rampant (especially since the genocide began). In 2022, the food security rate in Gaza was 65 percent (West Bank and Gaza, 2023). What does that mean? Over a million Palestinians didn't have enough food to feed their families. Even in the early days of 2023, 1.84 million Palestinians were on the verge of starvation.

- **Limited resources:** Gazans don't have access to many essential services, such as drinking water, a decent healthcare system, good schools, etc. Even though the Zionist media often blames the Gazans and Hamas for being incompetent (*Failing Gaza*, 2022), in reality, the fact that merely 4 percent of Gaza's water is drinkable and it is bordered by polluted seawater, is a consequence of the Israeli blockade.

- **Limited energy availability:** The blockade has also affected the energy supply in Gaza. As a result, a Gazan family used to get as little as two hours of electricity daily.

- **No basic materials:** Gazans also lack the basic materials required for construction, industry, and agriculture. This blockade makes life in Gaza very difficult.

How does the Blockade Affect the Gazan Infrastructure?

- **Water infrastructure:** The blockade prevents Gazans from constructing water infrastructure, so they don't have access to fresh water.

- **Electricity infrastructure:** Israeli military campaigns repeatedly target the energy sector. That's why there's widespread destruction in Gaza and a significant loss of electricity.

- **Commercial infrastructure:** It's estimated that Israel's military strikes wiped out over 200 industrial and economic facilities (Yasin, 2021).

- **Agricultural infrastructure:** The fishing zone also falls under several Israeli restrictions on what Gazans can and cannot do. For instance, thousands of Gazan fishermen aren't allowed access to 85 percent of the agreed fishing water. The parts that they can access are heavily polluted.

You may wonder how the international community responds to these atrocities. Clearly, Israel has always been an apartheid state where Jews live in privilege and Arabs are routinely discriminated against. "No-Arab" zones are in place, Palestinian students and workers suffer from racism in mainland Israel, and the people of Gaza are forced to somehow survive in abject misery. Don't Gazans get aid? Yes, the world does help them with aid, but it is often conditional and limited. The blockade also restricts the entry of aid, and the aid agencies themselves are often subject to Israeli restrictions or reliant on Israeli approval. The blockade is widely considered a violation of international law, specifically contravening the Fourth Geneva Convention, which prohibits collective punishment and the blockade of civilian populations. So, what has the international community done to attempt to help Palestinians?

International Diplomatic Efforts and UN Resolutions Regarding Gaza

> "Whether it's a child imprisoned by a military court or shot unjustifiably, or a house demolished for lack of an elusive permit, or checkpoints where only settlers are allowed to pass, few Palestinians have escaped serious rights abuses during this 50-year occupation ... Israel today maintains an entrenched system of institutionalized discrimination against Palestinians in the occupied territory." — Sarah Leah Watson, Middle East Director at HRW.

The region of Gaza came under Israeli military occupation in 1967, and the forces left forty years later. A casual observer would think that Hamas had been in control of Gaza since 2007; however, the Gaza Strip is besieged by Israel on all sides (as explained above). So, how is the international community responding to the ongoing humanitarian crisis? Even before the start of the Gaza Genocide, the world was engaged in diplomatic efforts to address the crisis. We have Amnesty International reports that described Israel as an apartheid regime in 2022 (Amnesty International, 2024). More recently, an independent probe into the conflict by the UN concluded that both Israel and Hamas were guilty of war crimes (Murphy, 2024). Let's examine how these communities and organizations have previously addressed this issue:

- **United Nations:** The General Assembly adopted a non-binding resolution in October 2023 (GA ES-10/21) that called for a humanitarian truce. In December, a similar resolution was passed, demanding a ceasefire in Gaza. This was supported by 153 countries and only ten countries opposed it. Unfortunately for Palestinians, the Security Council failed to adopt the resolution because of the Western states' opposition, working at the behest of Israel.

- **EU and the Arab League:** The ongoing genocide in Gaza has even compelled many European nations to cry out in horror and demand a ceasefire. For instance, French President Emmanuel Macron called an impromptu conference on the Gaza issue and also dispatched his intelligence chief to Beirut so he could negotiate a ceasefire with the Lebanese government. However, Macron's efforts are clouded in hypocrisy. Other European nations with genuine solidarity with Gazans are Ireland, Spain, Belgium, Norway, and Malta. They have called for the EU to pick sides and support a ceasefire. Also, the ongoing genocide of Gazans was a priority of the forty-seven-article Kampala Declaration proclaimed by the Non-Aligned Movement (NAM). Some Arab countries have even endorsed a proposal for an end to the Arab–Israeli conflict and have floated the idea of a UN-backed peacekeeping force to be deployed in the Strip post-withdrawal of Israeli forces.

- **International community:** Statistics show that most Americans now condemn Israel's atrocities in Gaza, and two-thirds of voters are asking for a permanent ceasefire in Palestine (Springs, 2024). Many countries have called for an immediate ceasefire and a de-escalation of hostilities. Various states have given their support to the idea of a two-state solution. The Holy See, Cuba, and many other countries in the world have spoken against the wave of violence and terrorism in Gaza. Notably, Brazilian President Luiz Inacio Lula da Silva has stated, "In Gaza and the West Bank, we are witnessing one of the greatest humanitarian crisis in recent history, now spreading dangerously to Lebanon." These states have also argued that the US government must be held accountable for its repeated complicit veto, which guarantees impunity for war crimes and crimes against humanity committed by Israel.

Sadly, however, the continuous efforts of the international community have fallen on deaf ears; their objections have not been heard, and their appeal to humanity remains unanswered. Where the international community has failed, Gazans still have an Absolute Authority to put their faith in: the Lord Almighty. The people of Palestine—be they Muslims or Christians—have trust in God. So now, we'll explore the role of religion and spirituality in the Palestinian culture. This will clear up any misperceptions and will help you understand just how important concepts like martyrdom and jihad are to Palestinians. "We love death more than you love life" is how Gazans respond to Zionists when the Israeli media portrays Palestinians' celebration of martyrdom as some sort of crazy obsession with death. We'll explain the Islamic fundamentals regarding *Qayamah* (Armageddon) and *Akhirah* (Hereafter). This accurate and unbiased discussion of concepts like jihad and martyrdom in Palestinian culture will provide sharp perspective of what Gazans value in this life.

7. Faith, Religion, and Spirituality in Gaza

"To God, we in Gaza are either martyrs or wit-
nesses to liberation, and we all wait to see where
we will be. We are all awaiting, oh God, your true
promise." — Heba Abu Nada's last Facebook post.

The pictures coming out of Gaza are usually pretty harrowing, depicting bloodied heads, kids missing limbs, and other unspeakable examples of Israeli atrocity. However, some pictures reflect hope and make the world look a little brighter again. In one such picture, Palestinians bow in prostration on the grounds of a now obliterated mosque. In the Rafah Camp, Palestinians continued to hold Friday prayers in the blessed month of

Ramadan. Since they couldn't locate a mosque that was still standing, they sought solace among the ruins of a place of worship that Israel had razed to the ground during 2023 offensive. Worshipers kneel in rows along the street by the remnants of the al-Farouk Mosque. They had laid out their prayer mats in the shade of a minaret, the sole remaining part of the mosque that was flattened by a godless army. These images reflect Gazans' courage and determination, as well as their willpower and strong desire to survive. Most importantly, it shows their attachment to their faith, a key difference between the Israeli and Palestinian societies. After all, almost 99 percent of Gazans are Muslims by faith! One survey indicated that 85 percent of Palestinians are deeply committed to their religion, and over 70 percent pray daily (Pew, 2012).

Religion and spirituality play a profound role in the lives of ordinary Gazans, fueling their struggle for the right of self-determination, survival against Israeli oppression, and ongoing resistance. The harsh realities of occupation and economic hardships haven't numbed a Palestinian's drive for the faith of Islam. In fact, Gazans find the message of hope in religious teachings. Religion tells them: *Inna Ma'al Usri Yusra* (No doubt, there is relief with hardship). They know that God has the best things planned for them, and if they have enough faith, they will be delivered from their hardships.

For Gazans (and, to some extent, most Muslims around the world), faith isn't personal; it is communal and part of their national identity. We've discussed the religious demographics of Gaza's population, but let's revisit several key facts about an average Gazan's religious identity:

- Islam and Christianity are the two dominant religions among Palestinians.

- Just as a huge majority of Gazans are Muslims, they subscribe to the Sunni Hanafi School.

- Shi'ism, Sufism, Salafism, and a few other Muslim denominations also exist in Gaza but don't claim a substantial following.

- The religious attitude of Gazans is conservative, where asking dead saints for help or recreational poetry/music is frowned upon by the religion.

- However, Gazans aren't exactly hardliners since they are tolerant of religious poetry or visiting a saint's shrine.

In short, the presence of different religious groups in Gaza is a testament to its diverse and complex religious life. From conservative individuals to liberal-minded people, average Gazans will always have a deep attachment to their faith. The role of faith in the Occupied Territories is not merely limited to individual piety but also extends to collective resistance and resilience.

In this chapter, we'll discuss the critical role religion—especially spirituality—plays in the life of an ordinary Gazan. How does religion shape Gazan culture? Then, we'll explore some of the most important sites in Gaza with religious and cultural significance. By the end of this chapter, you'll learn how Gazans exercise interfaith harmony among native Muslims, Jews, and Christians who harbor a collective hatred for their foreign occupiers and invaders, the Zionists.

Role of religion and spirituality in Gaza's society

"Gazans, like all believers, know even when facing a genocidal juggernaut that it is not the world's militaries, the media, the courts, human rights advocates, or so-called superpowers, but the Almighty alone who can protect them and has their affairs in His hands. He alone decides what is good for them. And so long as we hold on to our faith, all tests and trials are good for us." — Dr. Ovamir Anjum.

Gazans show that, with strong faith, a person can withstand all trials and tribulations. The experiences of the people of Gaza have faced wars, occupation, and tragedies beyond the horrors of WWII (even the Holocaust!). While many Jews gradually lost their faith in God and eventually turned into atheists due to their systematic extermination, the people of Gaza became even more steadfast in their faith. The ability to persist and resist despite the odds has become a symbol of hope and a source of inspiration for many around the world. The stories of individuals whose abiding faith has provided solace, strength, and hope even in the face of tragedy are a testament to the enduring power of spirituality in Gaza.

This sense of faith-derived hope is evident when a Gazan stands at the backdrop of fallen buildings, having lost everything but his family. Yet, he still says: "All praise to God." Or a mother praying for her deceased son by declaring, "My beloved son, Ibrahim, dearer to me than my *own* life! I send him now to his Creator who loves him." A man who lost both his children was found saying, "God creates us and takes us; he does what He wills. We will be patient, thanks to His grace and majesty." For a secular mind devoid of religious identity, the power of this faith is unknowable, something beyond imagination. For a godless mind (like the mind of Zionists), this very mindset is the major obstacle to their expansionist efforts—no matter how hard Israel tries, it can't prevent Gazans from fighting back. Gazans' faith in God is unwavering, so they always resist and never lay down arms. Their faith—this deep connection with God—makes them brave and **undefeated**.

Religious Leaders and the Key Role Clerics Play in Gazan Society

Known currently as the tragic victim of an ongoing genocide supported, paid for, and endorsed by the West, Gaza is much more than a mere strip of land bombarded by Israeli missiles; the religious history of this territory is much more complex and diverse. It's the birthplace of Imam al-Shafi'i, the progenitor of one of Islam's four canonical schools of thought (i.e., Hanafi, Maliki, Shafi'i, and Hanbali). The Great Omari Mosque lies in Gaza, dating back to the reign of the second Caliph of Islam and a trusted *sahabi* (companion) of the Prophet Muhammad, Umar b. al-Khattab (as the name indicates). This is where the Mamluks built the famous Mahkamah Mosque, a *madrassah* that issued religious education since its inception in the middle of the fifteenth century before Israel destroyed it.

Historically, religious leaders have played a crucial role in consolidating the community when a crisis strikes. They provide spiritual counseling to grieving Palestinians when they are denied the right to return to their olive trees. These leaders guide Gazan society and remind them of God's promise that the *good ending is for the God-fearing* (Q. 11:49) and *God's righteous servants shall inherit the Earth* (Q. 21:105). It's worth mentioning some of the most prominent leaders from Palestine to arise in the twentieth and the twenty-first centuries:

- **Amin al-Husseini:** He was the Grand Mufti of Jerusalem, one of the most important Gazans from the twentieth century. He played a key role in Palestinian nationalism as a leader of unwavering convictions. He was also one of the foremost supporters of the theory that both the British and the Zionists were oppressing the native Palestinians.

- **Taqiuddin al-Nabhani:** Besides being famous as the founder of Hizb, this Palestinian pan-Islamist scholar studied at al-Azhar and wrote a book detailing the principles of Islamic economics.

- **Ekrima Said Sabri:** Born in 1939, Sabri served as the Grand Mufti of Jerusalem before he was removed from this position in 2006. As a man of immense religious expertise, Israel has jailed him repeatedly since the beginning of the Gaza Genocide. Most recently, the corrupt regime of Israel detained him for mourning the death of Ismail Haniyeh.

- **Raed Salah:** Salah gained fame for his activism defending the Aqsa Mosque. The government of Israel has repeatedly sent him to jail on false charges of inciting hatred. Seen as the successor of Husseini, Salah has the spirit of a fighter, and Israeli oppression doesn't prevent him from speaking his mind about the persecution of Gazans (Masarwa, 2020).

- **Muhammad Ahmad Hussein:** He serves as the Grand Mufti of Jerusalem, staying active in the religious and political issues of everyday Palestinians.

- **Taissir Tamimi:** As the former judge of the West Bank's *Shari'ah Court*, Tamimi is still regarded as a cleric who participated in the country's social/political issues. He's one of the chief critics of Israel and does not shy away from speaking about Israel as a terrorist state.

Cultural preservation and heritage sites in Gaza

> *"Gaza is … a palimpsest of cultures, much of which has yet to be excavated … That heritage may never now be known because the shelling will have destroyed both what is below and above ground." —* Sarvy Geranpayeh, writing for The Art Newspaper.

During the forty-sixth meeting of the World Heritage Committee in India, the Palestinian embassy issued a mournful plea. If beheaded babies and their exploding skulls weren't enough for the world to break their silence, perhaps they would be moved by the mindless destruction of heritage sites in Gaza. The embassy requested that the fourth-century St. Hilarion Monastery be declared a World Heritage Site to ensure that bloodthirsty Zionists don't burn it to the ground (Vincent, P. 2024). Unfortunately, many Gazan historical sites have either been bombed to smithereens by Israel's inhumane offensive or sustained irreversible damage. Some of these sites include:

- Great Omari Mosque

- Greek Orthodox Saint Porphyrius Church

- Byzantine Church of Jabalia

- Shrine of Al-Khadir in Deir al Balah

- Blakhiya Byzantine cemetery

- Al-Saqqa House

- Sayed al-Hashim Mosque

Some of these names have been mentioned before. The first two sites were considered among the oldest-surviving relics of Gaza's past lives; the prestigious Omari Mosque (as explained earlier) dated back to Islam's infancy, while the Porphyrius Church was the third-oldest in human history. These aren't the only heritage sites that showcase Gaza as a melting pot of culture with a rich 4,000-year history of different religions, ethnicities, and civilizations, calling it their home. Gaza had the Rafah Museum, which housed a collection of ancient coins and copper plates, destroyed in October 2023. The Qarara Museum in Khan Younis was yet another casualty of the Israeli offensive, obliterating 3,000 artifacts dating back to the era of the Canaanites, the pre-Hebrew residents of Palestine.

Similarly, the Mathaf al-Funduq was a small Gazan museum that couldn't survive Israeli shelling and was destroyed in November 2023. The thirteenth-century Qasr al-Basha, formerly a castle, was turned into a museum, holding many artifacts from past civilizations. However, Zionists' wrath didn't spare this beautiful 800-year-old relic in December 2023. Even the Roman necropolis of Ard al-Moharbeen (i.e., the Land of the Warriors) was damaged beyond restoration by Israeli bombing.

The timeline of the destruction of Gaza's heritage reveals a clear, disturbing truth: Israel doesn't just want to erase Gazans from existence; it wants to eliminate any mention of them, resembling the tactic of every single genocide perpetrator in human history.

Who Bears the Blame? Implications and Accountability

Targeting these heritage sites is clear evidence of Israel's barbarity. The old Zionist motto, "A land without a people for a people without a land," shows that Zionist settlers were always commissioned by the devil to erase the existence of Palestinians (Alam, 2009). We witnessed the destruction of the heritage of Gaza back in 2014; ten years later, history is being repeated.

The destruction of Gaza's heritage has damaged the famous Ibn Uthman Mosque, a fair structure that has withstood the test of time since the fifteenth century until the Israelis destroyed it. Similarly, a very revered site called the Sayed Hashem Mosque—named after the great-grandfather of the Islamic Prophet who passed away in Gaza while on a business trip probably in the late fifth century—sustained damage due to Israeli shelling. Accountability for this destruction and devastation lies solely on Israel.

However, no matter how hard Zionists try, they will never be able to deny that Gaza is the paragon of interfaith harmony and tolerance. Before Zionism had taken over, Jews, Muslims, and Christians in Palestine coexisted harmoniously. Let's discuss this religious harmony in the final section of this chapter.

Interfaith initiatives and tolerance in Gaza communities

In 1922, the British Mandate conducted a survey revealing that 73,000 Christians lived in Palestine since Christianity began (Shephardson, 2023). In Bethlehem, the Palestinian Lutheran minister Munther Isaac designed the Nativity scene in his tiny church to resemble Jesus Christ as a small baby trapped under the rubble, dedicating the Christmas of 2023 to the persecuted people of his country, Palestine. His sermon, delivered just before Christmas, went viral in which he addressed the Christians living in Europe, saying: "I never, ever want to hear you lecture us on human rights or international law again!" His statement was a slap in the face of the Western liberals who defend Israel to their final breath and refuse to describe Israel's offensive in Gaza as a full-blown genocide (Robbins, 2024).

Palestinian Christians have always maintained a rich presence in Gaza, as history shows us. Today, most of them are Arab Christians, part

of the Eastern Orthodox Church. They fall under the Greek Orthodox Patriarch of Jerusalem, cut off from the majority Catholic/Prot-
estant Christendom. The difference between the Palestinian Christian
community from the rest of Christendom isn't unique; it dates back to
more than a thousand years when Palestinian Christians insisted that
Jesus only had a single nature and not two (one divine and another
human) like the Turkish Christians maintained.

They are also some of the most neglected victims of Israeli brutality. In
the events of 1948, some 75,000 Christians lost their homes. Muslims and
Christians living in Palestine share the common bond of facing, resisting,
and living to tell the tale of Zionist tyranny. As of 2017, 47,000 Christians
resided in the West Bank. On the other hand, the Gazan Christian population amounted to just over 3,000. However, Gazans aren't known to discriminate against their countrymen based on religious affiliation. They
play a crucial role in keeping the local economy alive, making the Palestinian economy thrive with their contributions. For instance, the ex-head
of Gaza's Catholic Church, Father Manuel Musallam, revealed in 2008
that one-third of the Gazan economy was controlled by Christians who
owned real estate in the territory. It is a testament to how well-ingrained
Christians are in Muslim society (Moussa, 2021).

When it comes to religious harmony and interfaith relationships,
a survey from 2020 shows that a great majority of Gazans considered their community well-integrated into Palestinian society! They
reported facing no discrimination from their Muslim neighbors.
Another study reported that Christians who lived in Gaza attributed
their mass emigration from Palestine to the effects of Israeli brutalities—discrimination from their Jewish overlords was what made them
flee the country.

> *"The pressure of Israeli occupation, ongoing con-*
> *straints, discriminatory policies, arbitrary arrests,*
> *confiscation of lands added to the general sense*
> *of hopelessness among Palestinian Christians." —*
> *Christians of Gaza and West Bank.*

This occupation led to a series of uprisings called the "Intifadas."

In the next chapter, you'll learn how Intifadas came to be, what justified them, and how they showcased Palestinians' undying spirit of resistance.

8. Israeli Occupation and Intifadas

"The ultimate tragedy is not the oppression and cruelty by the bad people, but the silence over that by the good people." — Martin Luther King.

In the middle of December 2023, the calls for *Intifada* began circulating online and became a topic of public discourse. Like always, Zionists misinterpreted these slogans as a "call for exterminating global Jewry" or "blatantly anti-Semitic chants" to discredit the genuine Palestinian activism for the freedom of their homeland! We had the likes of Elise Stefanik blatantly equating Intifada with the "genocide of Jews," which is simply wrong and a misrepresentation of the history of these uprisings that were meant to end the Israeli occupation of Gaza (Kuttab, 2023). However, Elon Musk—the stooge of global Jewry—was quick to ban such terms on X, formerly Twitter, and different countries—Germany being the foremost of them, not surprisingly—prohibited the usage of this term.

It was like when the Black Lives Matter movement that emerged in the wake of George Floyd's murder was discredited as a call for the extermination of the White race. Even today, White supremacists and the neo-Nazi (neo-fascist) groups in the United States dishonestly try to make Black activism seem violent and genocidal just to hide their *own* genocidal intent. Similarly, Zionists around the world try to portray terms like "Intifada" or chants like "from the river to the sea" as genocidal slogans, even though they are the ones who deny Palestinian nationhood.

Ever since the rumors of a *Third Intifada* started making waves in Israel in 2015, it was understood that the term "Intifada" meant rebellion of a massive scale, not a Nazi-like chant to kill all Jews. It's tragic and hilarious at the same time to notice that the phrase "From the [Jordanian] river to the [Mediterranean] sea" is deemed acceptable when used by fascists from the Likud party but a call for the extermination of Jews when used by Palestinians (Boffey, 2023). All these calls, chants, slogans, and demands are meant to end the occupation of Gaza—whether this goal is achieved via armed resistance or peaceful activism is beside the point.

You'll search the term "Intifada" online and see Jewish media trying to confuse readers by comparing this beautiful, powerful word with terrorism. One source that shall remain nameless says: "While the word "Intifada" might mean "uprising," in practice, it is violence against Jews. Calls for "Intifada" on the streets of Canada, or elsewhere, should always be understood as such." We can clearly see the lie here; "Intifada" means uprising and rebellion against occupation. If done against White oppressors or, shall we say, even Muslim oppressors, it'll, by no means, stand for a call for exterminating that particular race. In WWII, the Allies weren't trying to exterminate all Germans; when Native Americans fought back, they were not terrorists. The act of resistance by the oppressed against the oppressor, i.e., an Intifada, isn't an act of terrorism or genocide. History is replete with countless examples.

Have you ever heard of Nat Turner? In 1831, this enslaved person took his fifty followers and staged a revolt against their White masters, killing almost sixty individuals, including women and children. Even though he would be branded as a terrorist and child killer today, many Black activists revere him and call him a hero since he represented something much bigger than his actions: the will of the African-American race to regain their freedom and throw away the yoke of slavery (Wbur, 2016). By contrast, Hamas and other resistance movements focus on attacking Israel's military installments and IDF soldiers. The chant "From the river to the sea" doesn't stand for the mindless massacre of Jews but the destruction of Israel, a regime that uses apartheid as a weapon to subjugate Palestinians. Just as Nelson Mandela was called a terrorist even though he was a freedom fighter, *in reality*, Intifadas weren't acts of terrorism but genuine struggles for independence. It's worthwhile to look into these awe-inspiring stories of resistance.

In this chapter, we'll explore the history of Intifadas. What happened in the two Intifadas? Why did they even happen in the first place? What do we learn from them about Palestine and Israel? You'll learn how to answer the typical Zionist argument that "Intifada means killing all Jews" or "Israel isn't occupying Gaza anymore." So, keep reading and find out the truth behind Zionist lies!

Occupation of Gaza

Recently, the top court of the UN proclaimed that the Israeli presence in Palestinian territories must end since it was illegal and amounted to the occupation (Berg, 2024), as if the Palestinians needed reminding that their homeland was being occupied! Despite pro-Palestine activism receiving an endorsement from one of the highest legal authorities and claims that Israel left Gaza in 2005, Gaza is still occupied! Zionist leaders and activists claim that Gaza was given freedom in 2005 and that Arabs used this freedom to build bombs and attack Israel, implying that Arabs don't deserve freedom and have to be subjugated. It's amazing, albeit predictable, how occupying forces always try to portray the oppressed as "sub-humans" who are not worthy of liberation, just like most of Europe mocking the idea of freeing their Asian/African colonies.

Here's a brief recap of how Gaza came under Israeli occupation. After the Six-Day War of 1967, the evil regime of Israel occupied the Gaza Strip after defeating a coalition of Egypt, Syria, and Jordan. To the joy of all Zionists, Israel doubled its territory. For Palestinians, it led to widespread repression and displacement of Arab residents. This withdrawal led to the formation of organizations like Hamas.

After some forty years of brutal occupation, Israel decided to "disengage" from Gaza, a soft expression of the Zionist regime's decision to simply pull its military out of Gaza. All military forces were called back, and civilian settlements were dismantled in the summer of 2005. However, this withdrawal or disengagement was for show only. As Noura Erakat writes in *Justice for Some*: "Israel insisted its occupation had ended, but it also recognized that Gaza was not sovereign … it could deny Palestinians the right to fully govern themselves and simultaneously use military force to thwart their resistance to colonial domination." Gaza was declared a "hostile entity," ensuring that Israel didn't have any duty to protect the residents of Gaza without giving the residents the right to defend themselves via military or police. Some other ways that Israel maintained its occupation of Gaza without labeling it as "occupation" are as follows (Sanger, 2011):

- Policing Gaza's external land perimeter

- Exclusive authority in local air space

- Exercising security activity in the ocean off the coast

- Maintaining Israeli military presence on the Gaza-Egypt border

- Right to reenter Gaza at will (and restore formal occupation)

- Controlling six out of seven land crossings (Egypt controls the seventh)

- Controlling the movement of goods and persons

- Providing water, electricity, utilities, telecom, etc.

- Controlling the Palestinian Population Registry

In the everlasting words of the same Noura, Israel rebuffs the *de jure* application of occupation while maintaining effective control over Gaza and the West Bank. It is a recourse to police powers, which supports Zionist colonial expansion efforts and apartheid rule (Erakat, 2017). That's why Hamas came into power in 2007 and kept resisting Israeli occupation. This is a case of Intifada or rebellion against one's oppressors, something we'll explore in detail in the next section.

A Case for Intifadas

The West ruined the word "jihad" for us. That's what some Islam apologists said in a debate with ex-Muslims. The word "jihad" meant a kind of struggle that doesn't always have to be a battle fought between Muslims and non-Muslims. It can be any struggle that leads you away from temptation. If you're fighting off your alcoholism, you're *essentially* "waging a jihad" against addiction. However, the West is adamant that the term "jihad" means a holy war.

Similarly, the Western mind cannot comprehend how a term like "Intifada" can be used the same way as "crusade." The term "crusade" doesn't always mean a war between Muslims and Christians; it can be used to describe an internal battle or resistance against an evil thing. "Jihad" and "Intifada" are both used to describe resistance as well. In the context of Israel and Palestine, the term "Intifada" means struggling for freedom and ending the occupation.

Here's a simple breakdown of what Intifadas were. In the late '80s and early 2000s, Palestinians started to openly resist Israeli occupation of their homeland. This Intifada was *actually* an umbrella term, including different activities that ranged from strikes/demonstrations and nonviolent resistance to armed conflicts and suicide bombings. After all, the trend of bombings had already been introduced by Hezbollah in the early '80s when the Shiite cleric/militant leader, Imad Mughniyeh, allegedly staged the bombing of the US embassy in Beirut. However, keep in mind the story of Nat Turner to remember that an armed resistance leading to civilian deaths doesn't discredit the entire movement. Just as war crimes committed by a few soldiers don't discourage Americans from supporting their military, civilian deaths allegedly committed by Hamas militants or other random Palestinians during these Intifadas shouldn't prevent the world from supporting the genuine movement for Palestine's liberation.

Clearing Misconceptions Regarding Intifada

For Palestinians, Intifada is literally what it means: "Shaking off." I remember a student activist in the US who, trying to explain to a predominantly pro-Israel audience what Intifada means for Palestinians, said that if Taylor Swift had been an Arabic songwriter, she would've named her famous song *Shake It Off* as "al-Nafda Minhu" [النفض منه] because this is what the root of the Intifada, i.e., N-F-D, means; shaking something off you, such as brutal Israeli occupation. Some misconceptions regarding Intifada are in dire need of rectification. You should realize that:

1. They weren't all violent uprisings; most of the events staged by Palestinians during these uprisings were acts of civil disobedience and peaceful demonstrations.

2. These uprisings weren't some masterful plan to eradicate all Jews; Intifadas were barely planned, if at all. They were spontaneous outbursts and organized by different Palestinian factions with an array of political goals.

3. If any unethical actions were committed by demonstrators, such as terrorism or the deaths of civilians, those acts don't discredit the entire freedom movement. The majority of Palestinians don't support civilian deaths; they simply demand freedom from occupation.

You can better understand Intifadas by understanding the broader context of Palestinian resistance to the Israeli occupation; that's why we dedicated the previous seven chapters to all that and only discussed the history of Intifada in the eighth chapter. You can also compare the two Intifadas with the Indian movement of independence against the brutish British, the Algerian War of Independence against the fearsome French, the Korean War of Independence against the Juggernaut of Japan, or the South African struggle against the white-washed White apartheid. In the next section, we'll dive into the history of the two Intifadas.

Intifadas: A History of Resistance

"If any white man in the world says give me liberty or give me death, the entire white world applauds. When a black man says exactly the same thing word for word, he is judged a criminal and treated like one." — James Baldwin.

In the early fifties, the people of Iraq revolted against King Faisal II (who was eventually murdered in the late fifties) in an event called the Intifada. That's when this word slid into Palestinian vocabulary. Later, it was used during the events of the Arab Spring. By no means has the Intifada ever been a call for terrorism or violence against innocent people. It's most certainly not a call for the extermination of Jews. It's equally important to remember that the first Intifada was much more nonviolent than the second one. It's only the brutal Israeli response to the subjugation of peaceful demonstrations that led to the second Intifada being less nonviolent than the first one. In the words of Daniel Lefkowitz, a professor at the University of Virginia, the Intifadas were a movement of civil disobedience and protests characterized by:

- Work stoppages

- Boycotts and demonstrations

- Rocks or Molotov cocktails (rarely)

In his words: "It was the David-Goliath representation—stones against machine guns ... Intifada and genocide: To me, that's an unreasonable stretch!" But why did the two Intifadas take place? We've gone over the justification for Intifadas in the previous section. Here, we'll discuss the historical information available for these events. Remember, in the words of Daoud Kuttab, a person who witnessed the events of the first Intifada with his *own* eyes: "To equate the call for an end to the Israeli occupation with a call for the genocide of Jews is a bizarre reversal that turns victims into aggressors."

First Intifada

The "First Uprising" started in the last month of 1987. Against the backdrop of an Israeli truck clashing with a civilian vehicle and killing four Palestinians, Palestinians started an "uprising" against the occupying force of Israel. It was a grassroots movement that mainly involved acts of civil disobedience. As a result, Palestinian civilians staged strikes, boycotted Israeli products, demonstrated against their occupation, and—in rare cases—threw rocks at the occupying force. Israel responded by sending 80,000 troops into Gaza.

Like a scene out of a dystopian Hollywood movie showcasing the typical "rebel alliance" fighting a brutal, tyrannical regime, Palestinians kept resisting! However, Israelis used live ammunition and rubber bullets to subdue this uprising. While a hundred Israelis lost their lives, Palestinians suffered over 1,100 reported casualties. Thousands of them were either injured or jailed. Israeli soldiers used excessive force and repressive measures to counter the first Intifada. Here is a breakdown of how Israel acted like a typical tyrannical regime when dealing with these protests:

- Torturing prisoners and using excessive force against civilians

- Collectively punishing Palestinians by demolishing their homes

- Closing schools and restricting access to essential services in Gaza

The Result of the First Uprising

Here is how the First Intifada was a major success for the cause of the liberation of Palestine:

- **International Awareness:** The plight of Palestinians became a worldwide phenomenon. It exposed to the rest of the world an oppressed, victimized community and showed the harsh realities of living in Israel. Pictures of young Palestinians confronting Zionist soldiers sparked worldwide sympathy for this cause as the world witnessed the asymmetry of power and human rights abuses in the Occupied Territories.

- **Political Landscape:** After the Intifada, Hamas and Islamic Jihad emerged as military forces that swore to use armed resistance to push the Zionists out of Palestine. They became the alternatives to frail organizations like the PLO. Therefore, the PLO was motivated to eventually negotiate a future where the existence of Israel was recognized as a political reality.

- **Israeli Oppression:** These events also caused a shift in Israel's policy toward Palestine—even Jerusalem's civil society was influenced by it. The Zionist tyranny realized that Palestinians had, in the words of Ehud Barak, "become like a pillow. Every time you punch them, they return as though they were never punched."

Ultimately, the uprising set the stage for the Madrid Conference in 1991 and the subsequent Oslo Accords in 1993. These agreements aimed to establish a framework for peace and Palestinian self-governance, although they ultimately fell short of achieving lasting solutions. In 1993, Israel and PLO recognized each other when Arafat and Rabin shook hands on that historic day. However, two years later, Rabin was shot dead by a settler. After Rabin, the likes of Benjamin Netanyahu and Ariel Sharon multiplied their efforts to subjugate Palestinians by establishing more illegal settlements in the West Bank. These events led to the second Intifada in the early 2000s.

Second Intifada

By the winter of 2000, the events of the first Intifada had filled young Palestinians with an elevated sense of self-esteem (Baker, 1990). A political storm was brewing in Israel, however. Ariel Sharon, a very famous and ferocious right-wing activist from the Likud Party, visited the al-Aqsa Mosque in Jerusalem. Surrounded by a contingent of riot police. Even though Sharon was pretending that this was merely part of his political campaign—he was bidding for votes to become the Prime Minister—Palestinians saw it as a deliberately provocative move that challenged their religious and national identity.

The controversial visit barely lasted an hour, and Palestinian anger quickly escalated into violent clashes. Young men, fueled by a mix of indignation and fear, hurled stones and debris at the Israeli forces. The riot police responded with tear gas and rubber bullets, leading to injuries on both sides. The scene was chaotic, with shouts of "murderer" and chants of defiance echoing through the streets of Jerusalem. This moment marked the ignition of what would become known as the Second Intifada, a violent uprising that would last for several years. That's why this Intifada is also called the "al-Aqsa Uprising." It lasted for five years and witnessed both Israeli and Palestinian sides engaged in armed conflict.

Even though the visit of a butcher like Sharon—the man notorious for the Sabra and Shatila massacres—to Islam's third-holiest site was the last straw that broke the camel's back, historians believe that the second Intifada was caused by the failure of the Oslo Accords and Israel not maintaining its end of the deal. The expansionist activities of Sharon and Netanyahu were also responsible for this Intifada. Since the first Intifada, Palestinians had observed illegal settlements increasing and their territory shrinking. Palestinians, a study shows, had developed PTSD due to the array of violent actions committed by the IDF and even civilian settlers (Lavi & Solomon, 2005). Despite blaming military organizations like Hamas and PLO for attacking civilians during the second Intifada, the following illustrates how Israel was the primary aggressor:

- The ratio of Palestinians to Israelis killed was almost 20 to 1.

- Israel disproportionately used live ammunition and tear gas.

- Israel demolished 5,000 Palestinian homes and damaged 6,500 beyond repair.

- IDF carried out target killings of top Palestinian leaders that caused civilian casualties.

- The Separation Wall was seen as an act of collective punishment against Palestinians.

However, the second Intifada led to the end of the "formal occupation" of Gaza. It also marked a change in Palestinian leadership as Yasser Arafat died in 2004, replaced by Mahmoud Abbas as the new face who maintained a conciliatory stance in dealings withAriel Sharon. Under the supervision of Egyptian and Jordanian leaders, Sharon and Abbas ended the Second Intifada. However, these peace talks were futile as Abbas was in cahoots with the Zionist regime.

What's Next for Palestine? A Case for Armed Resistance

"Nobody in the world, nobody in history, has gotten their freedom by appealing to the moral sense of the people who were oppressing them." — Assata Shakur.

What's the future of the Palestinian resistance movement? What does the future hold for Gazans? Will they attain freedom or not? Will there be a third uprising? Only time can tell! Let's consider some statistics to bring the point home.

In the early years of the second Intifada, a study (Halileh et al., 2002) discussed the toll of conflict on the health of the Palestinian nation. This is what the study found:

- 58 percent of injuries were in young men aged eighteen to thirty-four years

- 25 percent of injuries were in school-age children

- 5 percent of injuries were in women

- 10 percent of injuries were in people over the age of fifty

Despite all the injuries and casualties, Palestinians are standing strong against Zionists. They are fighting and resisting, never surrendering. When the PA fails them, when the world disappoints them, they're still encouraged to fight by their faith, their belief in the Eternal Justice of the Almighty. This is why so many Palestinians support Hamas. Hamas is what happens when you brutalize a nation to a point where they see martyrdom as an escape from the horrors of living.

In the next chapter, we'll discuss Hamas in detail. What is Hamas, and why does it exist? Who are some of the leaders of Hamas? Why do Palestinians support Hamas? Why should Americans have sympathy for Hamas? We'll discuss it all in the much-awaited ninth chapter!

9. Birth of Hamas

"We know through painful experience that freedom is never voluntarily given by the oppressor; it must be demanded by the oppressed." — Martin Luther King.

As the month of October was finally bidding farewell to the residents of Khan Younis in 1962, just a few years before the infamous Six-Day War, a child was born to two Palestinian refugees who had to leave their ancestral home in Ashkelon due to Zionist atrocities. The little boy was raised in a refugee camp and witnessed how his people, the Palestinians—natives of the Holy Land—were discriminated against by occupiers from Eastern Europe. He grew up in poverty. There wasn't enough food in that crammed camp, a densely populated pseudo-city where every face had the shadow of a traumatic past.

His family struggled to make ends meet, often relying on UN relief work for basic services. Growing up, all that the boy knew was agony, anguish, and animosity from his blue-eyed, yellow-haired oppressors who treated Palestinians as sub-humans. It sounded so weird to his young ears when the Zionists claimed that they had "first dibs" on the lands of his ancestors, even though the Zionists hadn't lived here for a millennium! When he became an adult, he enrolled in the Islamic University of Gaza, where he met his future wife, an impressive *alimah* (female scholar) with a master's degree in theology. But the boy—now an amazing young man—had a different future planned in his head.

The discrimination that he and his fellow countrymen had faced, the stories of al-Nakbah that his parents recounted, and the harsh realities of everyday life that he saw with his very own eyes—all catalyzed him to become a revolutionary! In the eighties, he started participating in Islamist movements with the intention to wage *jihad* against the occupying regime and liberate his country from the clutches of imperialists. When he resisted, the Israeli forces sent him to jail, where he learned Hebrew and befriended numerous future freedom fighters. Known as a chief analyst of the Jewish people's history and a man with no mercy for those collaborating with Israel, he rose to prominence in a new military organization called Hamas. In August 2024, this man became the new leader of this movement.

This is the story of Yahya Sinwar—to be honest; this could be the story of any fighter resisting Israel and working toward the creation of a Free Palestine. When it comes to Hamas's new elusive chief, a critical question comes to mind: What is Hamas, and what does it want? You may wonder what this military organization that shocked the world on October 7th with its *Tufan al-Aqsa* (Storming the al-Aqsa) Operation wants. What are its goals and objectives? How does it operate? Moreover, you may think that Hamas fighters are terrorists hell-bent on the destruction of global Jewry and, to an extent, Western civilization.

Or are they?

That's why this chapter focuses on Hamas in depth. We've briefly discussed the rise of Hamas in Gaza when talking about the politics of Palestine and the local government of the Occupied Territories. Now, we'll look into the details of Hamas and finally reveal the truth about this organization with supporters and opponents around the world.

The Creation of Hamas: Phoenix out of Ashes

What is Hamas?

Hamas is a Palestinian political party and armed resistance movement based in the Gaza Strip. It started in 1987 during the First Intifada in response to increasing Israeli violence. What makes Hamas different is that it offered a religious alternative to the more secular Palestinian parties that were prominent for years under Chairman Arafat. Initially, Hamas was linked to Egypt's Muslim Brotherhood, but little time passed before it secured an identity of its own.

In 1992, Hamas established the well-known military wing, the *Ezz al-Din al-Qassam Brigades*, to fight and resist the Israeli occupation. During the Second Intifada, these brigades carried out several significant attacks against Israel, solidifying Hamas's role as a key player in the Palestinian resistance. It works under the principle that "the enemy understands only force, resistance, and Intifada," not appeasement efforts or peaceful activism (Hockstader, 2001). That's why Palestinians support Hamas, and Hamas is working for the greater goal of ending the apartheid regime of Israel.

How does Hamas operate?

Hamas consists of two main parts, i.e., a political wing and a military wing. While each serves different roles, they follow the same leaders at the top. The political wing handles governance and social services, whereas the military wing is responsible for armed actions. We've mentioned the Qassam Brigades above, which is the military wing. Let's briefly describe these two wings here:

Political Bureau

The political wing was headed by Ismail Haniyeh before his martyrdom. Now, Sinwar has been selected as the new chief of the political wing (Roth, 2024). This bureau sets the group's general policy.

Qassam Brigades

The military wing of Hamas was led by Marwan Issa and Mohammed Deif before they went missing, and Deif was declared dead by Israel. While Deif and Issa served as the army's leader and deputy leader, the famous Abu Obaida was the spokesperson of the Qassam Brigades.

You might have seen the videos of the masked individual serving as the primary communicator of these secretive *mujahidin* since 2007. In one video, he revealed that Israel orphaned 85 percent of his unit's members—a major reason why these fighters are fueled with passion to dismantle the illegitimate State of Israel.

As for Deif, one of the most-wanted men by Israel since the nineties, Israel killed his wife and their two small children in 2014. That's why Deif fights and leads the Qassam Brigades. However, with no news on the health and whereabouts of Deif (along with the assassination of Issa and Haniyeh), Sinwar is also the leader of both wings; he is the face of Hamas, the face of resistance, and the face of freedom for all nations.

Other Wings

The Shura Council is like the Parliament of Hamas. Saleh al-Arouri led it in the West Bank, while the now-chief Sinwar served as the leader of this *Shura* in Gaza. Since the death of al-Arouri in January, Khalil al-Hayya has replaced him as one of the top leaders of Hamas. Then there is Zaher al-Jabarin, the "CEO of Hamas," likely due to his management style (TimesofIndia, 2024). Regarding administrative affairs, Essam al-Da'alis has been serving as Gaza's Prime Minister since 2021. It is worth noting that he's one of the few Hamas leaders not sanctioned by the West (Flatley, 2023).

As a government, Hamas has provided remarkable services to Gazans that go unnoticed by the Western media because of their love for the ethno-fascist Zionist regime. Hamas has tried replacing the loose Israel-enacted drug laws in Gaza with Egyptian-modeled stricter ones that even recommend the execution of drug dealers. By efficiently policing the previous lawless streets of Gaza, Hamas succeeded in reducing the drug epidemic by 80 percent (Progler, 2010).

What Does Hamas Want? Goals and Objectives

"Due to the gravity and consequences of Hamas's use of terrorism as a tactic, all other aspects of Hamas, including its extensive social services programs and its role as a political party, are overshadowed and often ignored by policymakers. Others recognize the complexity of Hamas as an organization and suggest that Hamas will continue to transform itself into a full political party and eventually disarm and cease all violent tactics." — Krista E. Wiegand in "Bombs and Ballots."

What does Hamas want? When it comes to Muslims resisting foreign occupation, the Western media opts for broadcasting rumors and propaganda instead of the truth. Due to their obsession with Israel, many Western media pundits believe that Hamas will attack Europe or infiltrate America. They equate Hamas with ISIS and al-Qaeda—hell-bent on establishing a global Caliphate. Instead, Hamas has made its mission and plans for the future very clear. Its 2017 charter outlines current political goals, such as:

- Negotiating a long-term truce with Israel

- Ensuring that all Palestinian refugees have the right to return to their homes

- Establishing a temporary Palestinian state based on the 1967 borders encompassing the West Bank, including East Jerusalem and the Gaza Strip

However, Hamas views the creation of a Palestinian state based on the 1967 borders as a temporary measure. It doesn't recognize the legitimacy of Israel and advocates for the "full and complete liberation of Palestine, from the river to the sea." According to the 2017 charter, Hamas's struggle is against the Israeli state and the Zionist movement due to their occupation of Palestine, *not against Jewish people*. The charter also criticizes Israel for linking its actions to Jewish values. Quoting from the Charter:

> "... conflict is with the Zionist project, not with the Jews because of their religion. Hamas does not wage a struggle against the Jews because they are Jewish but wages a struggle against the Zionists who occupy Palestine. Yet, it is the Zionists who constantly identify Judaism and the Jews with their own colonial project and illegal entity."

The October Seventh *Tufan al-Aqsa* Operation also had ambitions and goals- it was aiming to:

- end the blockade of Gaza

- free the thousands of Palestinian prisoners held by Israel

- change the current situation where Israel continues its occupation

That's why Hamas's actions found strong support in Gaza and the West Bank. Surveys show that the offensive, genocidal response by Israel to the events of October 7, 2023, has changed the minds of many Gazans who previously disliked Hamas but have now become supporters (Byman & Duff, 2023). With the freeing of prisoners, Hamas has proven once again that Israel only understands the language of violence; that's why the PA's attempts to appease Zionists will be unsuccessful.

Hamas and the status of a "terrorist organization"

"But isn't Hamas mainly a terrorist organization?"

That's probably what many of you are thinking right now. It's been said that one man's terrorist is another man's freedom fighter. Consider India-Pakistan rivalries where the Hindu nation deems Kashmiri fighters terrorists, yet the Muslim state calls them heroes. Those sympathetic to Palestine's cause do not declare Hamas an evil terrorist organization, while Zionists consider it one of the vilest anti-Semitic organizations in the twenty-first century. Countries around the world regard Hamas differently. Therefore, Hamas's status as a terrorist organization can be considered in the following ways:

1. **Negative:** Countries like the US, Canada, Australia, New Zealand, and European nations deem it a terrorist organization.2

2. **Halfise:** Some countries (like New Zealand before February 2024) deem the military wing, i.e., the Qassam Brigades, as a terrorist organization.

3. **Neutral:** Most countries in the world don't regard Hamas as a terrorist entity, such as Brazil, China, Turkey, Norway, Afghanistan, etc.

4. **Positive:** Some countries view Hamas positively, such as Algeria, Syria, Iran, and Muslim residents of India, Pakistan, and Bangladesh.

Hamas has also found allies in other militant entities, such as Hezbollah, that are also called terrorists by the West. That's why Hezbollah and Hamas cooperate. In fact, Hezbollah's leader congratulated Hamas on carrying out the Storming of al-Aqsa Operation as well (Khoury, 2023).

Hamas and Israel: Does Hamas Negotiate with Israel?

What is the nature of the relationship between Hamas and Israel? Why do some people accuse Hamas of being a party working for Israel? The allegations of the Hamas-Israel alliance are not founded in truth. Instead, they stem from a grave misunderstanding of Israel's policy toward Hamas. Netanyahu once thought that he could use Hamas to sabotage the Two-State Solution and weaken Palestine's movement for liberation (Nuki, 2023). This policy backfired when Hamas did not allow Zionists to use it to manipulate Palestinians.

It's a prime reason why Zionists are so fearful of Palestine because, unlike Mahmoud Abbas, they could not use Haniyeh or Sinwar to play their mind games. Hamas always stands its ground and sticks to its goals; it doesn't allow itself to be corrupted. Although the Jewish media presents Hamas as a bloodthirsty group of terrorists, it's Israel that has never accepted Hamas's peace offerings. Israel continuously attempts to eradicate any powerful political representation of Palestine. That's why it has refused to agree to peace deals brokered by the United States. Some examples are:

- Hamas considers armed struggle as just one of many tools to end apartheid and occupation, alongside diplomacy.

- In 2006, for the *Guardian*, Hamas leader Ismail Haniyeh disclosed that Israel turned down Hamas's proposal for a truce.

- In 2008, former Hamas chief Khaled Mesha'al offered a decade-long truce in exchange for the establishment of a sovereign Palestinian state along the 1967 borders with Jerusalem as the capital. However, Israel rejected this proposal.

- In 2015, Hamas offered a long-term truce in exchange for simply ending the Gaza Blockade, but Israel rejected it.

- In 2018, Haniyeh revived this offer by sending a handwritten letter in Hebrew to Israeli Prime Minister Netanyahu. Israel rejected it again.

Israel repeatedly rejected Hamas's diplomatic initiatives because it saw no reason to end the oppressive status quo, which it believed gave it power over Palestinians with minimal downsides. Israel's benefits outweighed the costs; Hamas is trying to change that (Kmaneck & Kmaneck, 2024). That's why Hamas is in Palestine, and everyone loves these soldiers. Don't think that Hamas is the first of its kind. History offers many parallels between Hamas and other famous revolutionary organizations.

For seven decades, extending an olive branch from the oppressed to the oppressor has never yielded results. In the meantime, settlers continued to occupy the West Bank. In his 1974 speech at the UN General Assembly, Yasser Arafat said:

> "I appeal to you to enable our people to establish national independent sovereignty over their own

land. Today, I have come carrying an olive branch
in one hand and a freedom fighter's gun in the other.
Do not let the olive branch fall from my hand. Do
not let the olive branch fall from my hand. War
flares up in Palestine, and yet it is in Palestine that
peace will be born."

The Likenesses of Hamas in Human History

Whether it is the Senussi Sufi order of Tunis, Omar al-Mukhtar of Libya, or Mahdi of Sudan, whenever a Muslim revolutionary challenges Western imperialism or fights European invaders, he is dubbed a *jihadi* terrorist. Whenever someone challenges the status quo and pushes occupiers out of the country, that man automatically becomes the beholder of the label "terrorist." There have been many organizations in world history that have used armed struggle against occupiers just like Hamas is doing, such as:

- The Algerian National Liberation Front struggled against the French and ultimately liberated the country after 200 years of European occupation.

- The Irish Republican Army remained active in the twentieth century, and their terrorist activities finally led to the famous Good Friday Agreement of 1998.

- The Palestine Liberation Organization used Hamas-like tactics against Israel and was founded in the sixties (when Hamas's senior leaders were little boys).

- Tamil Tigers fought for the creation of a Tamil state and introduced tactics like suicide bombing to the world; however, their activities weren't that successful.

- Colombia's Revolutionary Armed Forces started fighting the government in the sixties, and a peace agreement was reached in 2016.

- Organizations like Hamas often emerge in response to systemic oppression and violence faced by their communities. These militant entities argue that armed struggle is a vital means of resistance *when peaceful methods fail to yield results.* Such groups often claim to represent marginalized voices and seek to mobilize their populations against perceived injustices. For example, we saw the rise of the Viet Cong. These soldiers fought the Americans and eventually won. Just like the Taliban, they successfully thwarted the threat of US occupation. Fidel Castro and the Mexican Zapatistas are other examples of armed resistance used to overthrow tyrannical regimes.

A Case for Political Violence

Several philosophers and political theorists argued in favor of violent revolution as a means to political change. Even though violence against civilians isn't justified, armed resistance against governments has found acceptance in various philosophical circles, such as:

- **Karl Marx**: Advocated for the overthrow of capitalist systems through revolution, believing that the working class must rise against the bourgeoisie

- **Frantz Fanon**: In *The Wretched of the Earth*, Fanon argued that violence is a vital and cathartic response to colonial oppression

- **Mao Zedong**: Mao's theories on guerrilla warfare emphasized the necessity of armed struggle in the context of revolution, particularly in agrarian societies

- **Che Guevara**: Promoted the idea of revolutionary violence as a means to achieve social-political change while emphasizing the role of the guerrilla fighter

Hopefully, you can now see why Hamas's resistance is justified. In the face of state-sponsored violence, it becomes necessary to speak up and meet violence with violence.

Misconceptions Answered

Does Hamas Control Gaza?

Not totally. While Hamas manages local affairs within Gaza, Israel exerts significant control from the outside through its blockade. Israel forcibly controls:

- Airspace

- Sea access

- Movement of all goods and people in and out

- Telecommunications networks

- Electromagnetic spectrum

- Tax distribution

- Population registry

- Water supply

- Electricity and fuel

Hamas began governing Gaza in 2007 and has since managed:

- Healthcare

- Education

- Infrastructure

- Social welfare

- Law enforcement

- Public employment

Hamas is not a sovereign government. Israel's blockade prevents Palestinians from independently exercising control over Gaza's population, development, and economy. Notably, this blockade significantly limits the autonomy and self-determination of the people in Gaza. On the one hand, Hamas was democratically elected by voters in 2006, gathering momentum and earning votes in the West Bank and Gaza for its social services and resistance efforts.

Today, the two largest parties, Fatah and Hamas, are roughly tied, each enjoying the support of a third of the Palestinians. On the other hand, many Palestinians criticize Hamas's political wing due to its repressive policies and that the last elections were in 2006. However, 43 percent of Palestinians in the West Bank and Gaza believe that no party represents Palestine.

Does Hamas Speak for Palestinians?

The other polled Palestinians were split between parties, with no clear winner. While I have no statistics for Palestinians in the heartland ("Israel") or diaspora, like me, I can tell you that the global community largely supports Palestinian rights. Yet Hamas is currently the only group advocating armed resistance, which is widely supported. So, even though most Palestinians might not support Hamas as a party, the overwhelming majority support acts of resistance in general, whether by Hamas or others.

Hamas is just one of the many political factions within the Palestinian community. Remember Fateh, Arafat's group? It was the largest and initiated the resistance movement, with a significant presence across various Arab countries, a presence in Amman and Kuwait, and a large militia presence in Lebanon.

That's why we can say that Hamas *does, indeed,* talk and speak on behalf of Palestinians.

Is Hamas a Proxy of Iran?

No, Hamas operates independently with its own political agenda and military strategy, separate from Iran's influence. Even though Hamas and Iran maintain a strategic alliance characterized by financial, military, and political support from Iran, Hamas makes decisions based on its own interests. It manages relationships with other countries, such as Turkey, Qatar, and Egypt.

For instance, in 2012, Hamas severed ties with Syria due to its opposition to the Assad regime's violent suppression of protests, despite this decision causing tension with Iran, a staunch supporter of Assad. Is Israel a proxy of the US? Remember, anyone against the interest of the US in the ME is a proxy of someone else! Regarding Operation *al-Aqsa Flood*, Israeli officials acknowledge that there is no evidence linking Iran to the operation. In fact, Iran was caught off guard by it. Hamas independently coordinated and launched the operation to pursue its own objectives, as mentioned earlier.

Is Hamas Risking Palestinian Lives?

The West often point fingers at Hamas for killing Palestinians in their struggle against apartheid, inviting a deadly Israeli crackdown. However, the blunt reality is that Israel's blockade has claimed lives throughout Gaza before.

Of course, Palestinians have paid a devastating toll during this ongoing genocide. Yet, if it means paving the way for lasting change—breaking the siege and attaining freedom—it's a bitter pill many find themselves compelled to swallow. Ultimately, Palestine deserves more, in my opinion. It's undeniable that the people of Gaza are bleeding, but the blockade has obliterated any chance for peace.

Blaming Hamas for Israel's violence against Palestinians is unjust. Such an argument shifts blame onto the victims for resisting apartheid while pardoning the oppressors of their responsibility, essentially normalizing the mass killing of women and children as a "normal" Israeli response. Ultimately, supporting Palestinians doesn't necessitate endorsing Hamas as a political entity.

Hamas has institutions, ministries, student movements, and women's movements and employs thousands of doctors, teachers, judges, and aid workers. Whether you approve or not, Hamas has become ingrained in the fabric of Palestinian society, a historical fact that will endure. So, while you don't need to support Hamas to support Palestine, *you cannot oppose oppression without supporting the resistance to it.*

You cannot support freedom while supporting Israeli efforts to wipe out those who fight for that freedom, including Hamas, to leave Palestinians to defend Palestine. The Palestinian Authority in Ramallah (Abbas and PA leadership in the West Bank) had voiced its objection to Hamas forming a government in the Gaza Strip. The reality is that the power struggle in the West Bank could tilt unfavorably for the Palestinian Authority if Hamas gains popularity. Interestingly, despite limited resources, Hamas has garnered respect for its resilience, reflecting a deep-seated faith. Despite efforts by the US and EU to undermine Hamas using various means, the question remains: How do you defeat an ideology?

Are Hamas Leaders Billionaires?

Many Zionist journalists have pushed this narrative that top Hamas leaders are billionaires who live in luxury in Qatar (Vincent & Weinthal, 2023). These allegations are a decade old, and there has been zero evidence of this "secret wealth" of Hamas leaders. While it's true that Netanyahu's son is living a rich life in Miami while his countrymen suffer, Hamas leaders have shared their countrymen's sufferings.

It's the Israeli government that has created this rumor that all senior Hamas commanders are hiding their wealth in Qatar (show any paper trails much?). Mainstream media uses Ofir Gendelman as the person who propagated this "news" in Western media. That's the same guy who popularized the very infamous (and utterly disgusting) "Pallywood" conspiracy theory that states that all Palestinians are lying about their children's deaths. According to my research, the originator of this allegation is an individual who goes by Moshe Elad. He formulated this theory that Gaza is poor not due to the Israeli blockade—the prime reason why Gaza is said to still be occupied by Zionists—but Hamas leaders hoarding the wealth of Gaza in their luxury mansions.

There is currently no verified source that can tell us about the true net worth of the likes of Mashal, Yahya Sinwar, or the (late) Ismail Haniyeh. But it's 100 percent false that they are or ever were millionaires.

What's Next: War or Peace?

> "I mean, the oppressor is always in favor of law and order because it's his law and his order. He uses violence to maintain his position and calls it the rule of law. But when the person underfoot uses violence to change his status, he's called a criminal and a terrorist, and the violence of the State is called upon to put him down, and once again, it's called the rule of law." — Ramon in Margaret (2011).

Regardless of your stance on the matter, the assassination of Ismail Haniyeh was clear evidence that the Zionist regime isn't interested in peace talks or negotiations that may lead to a ceasefire in Gaza. We had a chance to bring Israelis and Palestinians to the table for peace talks. With Haniyeh out of the way, the window of opportunity to avert this catastrophe is rapidly closing.

The power to stop this descent into chaos lies in our will to resist the madness being orchestrated by those who seek to reshape the world through violence and domination. We must recognize that this conflict isn't just about territorial ambitions or political power; it's about the very essence of humanity. The atrocities being committed, the lives being shattered, and the future being threatened demand that we stand up and speak out. Silence and inaction only embolden those who wish to see the world burn for their twisted vision of supremacy.

Now is the time to rise against the manipulation and lies, to demand accountability from our leaders, and to insist on a path that leads to peace and justice, not war and destruction. The consequences of failing to do so will be felt by generations to come, as the seeds of hatred and division sown today will grow into an uncontainable wildfire tomorrow. We must act with urgency, for our collective future depends on it. Our voices, our actions, and our solidarity are the only tools we have to prevent the escalation of this conflict into a full-scale global war. The choice is ours: Stand by and witness the world descend into chaos or fight for a future where peace, dignity, and human rights prevail.

So, what's next for Hamas? What does the future hold for Palestinians? We have discussed Hamas as the primary resistance movement in the Occupied Territories. But is peace never an option? In the hands of competent leaders (unlike the folks from PA), peace can *indeed* be a valuable weapon. In the next chapter, we'll discuss the prospects of peace by the likes of Dr. Mustafa Barghouthi. Rest assured (and don't be alarmed by the fact that *Houthi* is his name), this chapter will show that peace activists do indeed exist and are pursuing a nonviolent solution to the Israel-Palestine problem.

10. Prospects of Peace and Reconciliation

"Peace does not mean an absence of conflicts. Differences will always be there. Peace means solving these differences through peaceful means—through dialogue, education, knowledge, and through humane ways." — The Dalai Lama.

There's a story of two WWII veterans who befriended each other while passing their final days in a small assisted living facility in Virginia. Being in their eighties and nineties, they spent time swapping their life stories, talking about the war and the enemies they fought. However, an awkward silence fell over as one veteran revealed that he had *actually* fought on the other side. You see, Buhrdorf manned an anti-aircraft gun for the Nazis, while Williams was an Allied pilot, dropping bombs on Germans. They were enemies, trying to kill each other back in the forties. Now, they are buds who have learned to set their past grievances aside and understand each other (Itkowitz, 2016).

We have countless examples of brutal enemies and rival nations that moved on to become allies. The US and the UK, Germany and France, Japan and South Korea, Iran and Iraq, etc.—many nations have learned to *give peace a chance*. But is something like that possible for Israel, especially since Israelis have turned into extreme fascists who want nothing else than the total extermination of Palestine? As Israel makes a move into the West Bank (a territory they menacingly call "Judea and Samaria"), can Palestinians ever live in peace with their Jewish occupiers?

Despite decades of conflict and mistrust, efforts to achieve peace between Israelis and Palestinians persist. Diplomatic initiatives, such as the Oslo Accords and the Arab Peace Initiative, have sought to establish a two-state solution based on mutual recognition and security guarantees for both Israelis and Palestinians. However, progress has been slow, with obstacles including settlement expansion, violence, and political divisions hindering negotiations. The crux of the matter is this: Israel wants a demilitarized Palestine and insurance that there would be no resistance against the status quo. What Israel is looking for is a subdued Palestine that isn't capable of defending itself against the occupation. However, Palestinians want Israel to let them go back to their lands, i.e., the Right of Return (ROR) or حق العودة (Haqq al-Awda al-Falastini). Without Palestinians returning to their homeland, there can be no peace!

The international community also plays a crucial role in facilitating peace and reconciliation in Gaza and the broader Israeli-Palestinian conflict. Today, via diplomatic efforts, humanitarian aid, and support for Palestinian state-building, countries and organizations seek to address the root causes of the conflict and promote a just and lasting resolution. We have examples of the United Nations and Amnesty International condemning illegal Israeli settlements in the West Bank. Israel has been declared an apartheid state, too. It means that there's an international resistance against Israel's ethno-fascism. Unfortunately, however, the response of the international community is weakened by the Western nations' unconditional support for Israel. Since any criticism of Israel is deemed an attack on global Jewry, the West remains silent over the genocide of Palestinians.

So, in this article, we'll discuss the peace initiatives by Palestinians. You'll know about peace activists who want to coexist with Israelis. We'll explore Dr. Mustafa Barghouthi's peace initiative and learn how PLO or Hamas have previously proposed peaceful solutions to the

Israel-Palestine issue. This chapter will give an overview of how peaceful initiatives have failed to resolve this problem, mainly because the tyrannical regime of Israel simply refuses to budge on several vital bottlenecks, such as the Right of Return. Hence, Israel's dishonesty and hypocrisy have made peace so difficult to achieve.

The Pathway to Peace and Progress

Experts have proposed different solutions to resolve this issue. I don't agree with all of these proposals, but it seems appropriate to mention them all here. One of the most popular solutions was the **Two Bridges to Peace**, a proposal that addressed both humanitarian needs and long-term political solutions to the case of Israel and Palestine. Here is a description of the two bridges (which are basically two stages for the sake of achieving permanent peace in Palestine):

- **First Bridge:** The goal of the first stage is to turn Gaza from a war-ridden territory to a healthier and better place. It involves the demilitarization of Gaza, i.e., eliminating Hamas or dismantling its military capabilities. Also, international oversight can ensure that Hamas doesn't regain its military capacity by monitoring aid and reconstruction efforts. Then, an interim government shall be formed to manage critical services and infrastructure.

- **Second Bridge:** In this phase, Palestinian statehood will be achieved by garnering support from Arab nations. International organizations will reduce Israeli fears of a hostile state. Also, it will be ensured that Hamas doesn't restore its public appeal among Gazans. No new governance structure in Gaza will incorporate Hamas or similar paramilitary organizations.

You can see the flaws in this approach. Here's why I believe this proposal won't work:

- It goes too far in focusing on and prioritizing Israel's national interests. As a genocidal regime, Israel doesn't have any right to have its "fears" heard. Imagine the Apartheid South Africa asking to demilitarize the Black opposition groups and military organizations.

- Demilitarization is simply an excuse to remove all opposition to Israel. Gaza was militarized for a simple reason: Israel's policy of discrimination against and suppression of Arabs. The best way to demilitarize Gaza is to subdue Israel and prevent its genocidal campaign. Imagine asking the Black Panthers to demilitarize instead of doing something about racist cops.

- Thirdly, I believe that Israel focuses too much on eradicating Hamas and less on changing how its fascist policies led to the formation of Hamas. If Israel had not been mistreating and massacring Arabs, there would've been no Hamas. Hamas exists because Palestinians are threatened by Jews. The dismantling of Israel will lead to peace in the Middle East.

I would like to dedicate an entire section to Dr. Mustafa Barghouthi. But first, we familiarize ourselves with other names in the peace process, i.e., the most famous peace activists from Palestine.

Peace Activists from Palestine

In 2021, a survey by the *Times of Israel* showed that most Israeli-Jewish youth hated Arabs and supported their expulsion. In 2016, only half of them wanted Palestinians expelled. Is peace possible with these individuals? For some Palestinians, it is! Here are the names of brave Palestinians trying to bridge the gap and find peaceful solutions to the Gazan Genocide:

- **Ali Abu Awwad:** He founded a movement called *Taghyeer* that hopes to bring peace. He's also a co-founder of *Roots*, a joint venture or peacemaking group among Israeli Jews and Arabs. Ali's biography heartbreaking. He was shot by soldiers, spent four years in jail, and lost his brother to Israeli violence (Rice, 2023). But he's still hopeful that one day, Israelis and Arabs will live in harmony.

- **Muhammad Kundos:** Then, we have Kundos, the founder of a school in Israel that teaches Arab and Jewish kids side by side. He says that, as Islamic and Jewish cultures have a lot in common, we can use these shared elements to bring peace to Palestine. From his perspective, the first step toward peace-making is to educate young children from the very beginning.

- **Rula Hardal:** As the CEO of *A Land for All*, Hardal believes Israel and Palestine should become two states. Her organization wants to base the Two-State Solution on the EU model, in which both countries would fall under a shared confederacy.

- **Rami Aman:** As one of the critics of Hamas, Aman is the founder of the *Skype with Your Enemy* initiative. In this initiative, Israelis and Palestinians have video chats with each other so they can better understand the opposite side's perspective. However, he criticized the Gazan Genocide and argued that Israeli atrocities would only lead to the emergence of more Hamas-like groups in Gaza (Davis, 2023).

- **Hamza Awawde:** Awawde strives to bring peace to Palestine and help Israeli Jews engage in conversations with Arabs. He believes that mutual respect, dialogue, and effective communication can make Israel and Palestine work toward regional peace.

However, all these activists pale in comparison with the efforts of the respected Mustafa Barghouthi. A distant cousin of Marwan Barghouthi, Dr. Mustafa Barghouthi has made a name for himself as a genuine proponent of peace. He is someone who can go toe-to-toe with Israeli academics in defense of why Palestinians should be free. While his cousin, Marwan, became disillusioned with the prospects of peace with Israel, Dr. Barghouthi kept pushing for a nonviolent solution to this problem. Let's discuss his Peace Initiative at length.

Dr. Mustafa Barghouthi's Peace Initiative

As of this writing, the presidential elections loom over Americans' heads, which begs the age-old question: *Why is our choice limited to Democrats or Republicans? Why isn't there a third option?* Even though Dr. Jill Stein is available as a third option as a Jewish woman who opposes Israel. Similarly, the people of Palestine who were tired of the dichotomy between Hamas and Fatah found a third option in the shape of المبادرة الوطنية الفلسطينية or the Palestinian National Initiative (PNI), headed by Dr. Barghouthi.

Co-founded by Dr. Barghouthi, PNI has worked toward a peaceful resolution of the Israel-Palestine case. The second Intifada was the catalyst for the emergence of this organization, which calls itself a nonviolent, secular Intifada. The locals know it as *al-Mubadara al-Wataniyah al-Falastiniya*, a third option that does not take the military approach to the Israel-Palestine issue. PNI's goals and objectives are:

- Ending the Israeli occupation

- Creating a sovereign Palestinian state

- Giving Palestinians the Right of Return

- Releasing prisoners entrapped in Israeli jails

- Mobilizing support for their cause internationally

PNI is a democratic coalition open to everyone, whether they are secular left-winged or oriented toward religion. Even though Barghouthi has been detained by Israelis for the false allegations of "disturbing the Zionist peace," he remains firm that nonviolence is the only way forward for Palestinians. We may even call him the true MLK of Palestine. When asked why he chose nonviolence and resisted Hamas-like jihad efforts to liberate Palestine, he responded by saying:

> *"It works better because it allows everybody, and not just a small group of people, to participate. It works better because it does not allow the Israelis to claim that they are victims in this conflict. It reveals and exposes them as they are in reality: the oppressors, the occupiers, and the creators of an apartheid system." (Rassbach, 2012)*

As a critic of the corrupt politicians of PA, he believes that nonviolence is the only way for Palestinians to achieve peace. In 2004, he ran for president by proclaiming that he supported the Two-State Solution if the newly emerged Palestinian state was founded on pre-1967 borders, peace with Israel, East Jerusalem as the capital, and the Right of Return for al-Nakbah refugees. He's a man of conviction who does not shy from criticizing the apartheid regime of Israel for persecuting Arabs. As a vehement critic of Fatah, he still believes that Hamas should be included in the peace dialogue since, quoting the great Dr. Barghouthi, *"Violence, extremism, fundamentalism, and suicide attacks are symptoms of occupation, oppression, and injustice."*

However, even this champion of peace lost hope in the possibility of an Israeli-Palestinian alliance. In an interview given in 2013, Dr. Barghouthi stated that the increase in illegal Jewish settlements in Palestine and the internal rivalries between Hamas and Fatah have frozen the peace process. In 2024, Dr. Barghouthi showed his utter disgust for the ongoing genocidal campaign in Gaza, calling it *a blatant example of a Zionist plan to eradicate Palestinians in the guise of fighting Hamas* (Perelman, 2024). In their *own* words, it's *"practically a war of a mighty Israeli army on the civilian population."*

The Role of the UN and Neighboring Countries

International actors also play a role in bridging the gap between Israelis and Palestinians. That's why we will discuss the efforts of the United Nations and neighboring countries to resolve this problem:

- **United Nations Organization:** The UN has passed many resolutions to establish peace in Israel-Palestine. In 1947, the UN passed Resolution 181, which proposed creating two states in the region. In Resolution 242, the UN called for Israel to withdraw from the Occupied Territories. Similarly, we can't ignore the role of UNRWA (the UN Relief and Works Agency) in bringing aid to Arabs. Maligned as a terrorist activity by Zionists, UNRWA has played a crucial role in protecting and nourishing civilians.

During the Gazan Genocide, the Secretary-General of the UN has called for a ceasefire multiple times.

- **Neighboring Countries:** On the other hand, neighboring countries have proposed solutions too. For instance, the Arab Peace Initiative of 2002 offered normalization of ties between Arab states and the Jewish nation if Israel withdrew from occupied lands. Egypt and Jordan have also kept a friendly stance toward Israel, acting as a broker in ceasefire negotiations after 10/7. Regional actors have also emphasized the need for a unified Palestinian Authority to represent Palestinian interests effectively.

However, these peace initiatives have all failed. In the next section, we'll look into the reasons why peace never worked out between Israel and Palestine. Then, you'll learn which party is *actually* responsible for keeping Palestinians repressed and causing chaos in the Middle East.

Challenges to Peace and Reconciliation

The world wasn't shocked when Israeli PM and the Butcher of Gaza, Benjamin Netanyahu, said that there would never be a Palestinian state as long as he was in power (Graham-Harrison & Helm, 2024). It's seen as a commonly known fact that neither the US nor Israel is serious about granting statehood to Palestinians, since a sovereign Palestine is deemed a threat to the existence of Israel. Let me say it again but bluntly: The very idea of treating Palestinians as equals is unacceptable to Israelis. They have become so mad in their hatred for Palestinians that they are not ready to treat them as human beings. That's why peace does not seem easily achievable in Palestine. Some other reasons why peace hasn't been achieved are:

- **Entrenched Distrust:** Palestinians haven't recovered from the memories of al-Nakbah, and view Israelis with mistrust. A long history of occupation, and over 75 years of brutal repression, have made them skeptical of Israel's willingness to bring peace to the Middle East. It's funny how Jews, who don't want the world to forget the horrors of pogroms and the Holocaust, expect Palestinians to just forget what happened to them and shake hands with Israel. It's just like how black people in the US are expected to just forget that slavery ever happened!

- **Political Divisions:** The current political landscape in Palestine is fragmented. The Hamas-Fatah split and the existence of rival organizations have prevented Palestinians from gathering under a single leader. Getting a unified representation in negotiations isn't possible either. These divisions hinder collective action and compromise since each party has unique objectives, strategies, and plans for the future of Gaza.

- **Competing Territorial Claims:** Israel keeps forming illegal settlements in the West Bank. Also, the status of Jerusalem remains controversial. Right-wing elements in Israel want to transform the Holy City (or the *Bayt al-Muqaddas* for Muslims) into another Temple, while Muslims wish for it to stay the al-Aqsa Mosque. These territorial claims have become a significant impediment to any potential peace agreement.

- **Security Concerns:** Israel claims that it has security concerns regarding the military capabilities of Hamas. Using Hamas as an excuse, Israel collectively punishes Gazans, creating resentment in the Arab community. The ongoing blockade and military operations further alienate Palestinians who wish to live in peace with Jews. That's why Palestinians have come to believe that the very existence of a "Jewish state" in their homeland is a threat to their freedom and well-being.

- **Humanitarian Crisis:** Whenever Zionists say, "… but October Seven happened," we should just remind them that one day before 10/7, journalists regarded 2023 as the deadliest year for kids in the West Bank (Muaddi, 2023). For the last seven decades, all Palestinians have been living under siege. Israel limits their access to health, learning, employment, and — since 10/7 — access to clean water. That's why Gaza has become a breeding ground for extremism and violence. This violence is a very reasonable response to occupation.

You may wonder: *What have PLO and Hamas ever done to resolve their issues with Israel nonviolently?* A cursory glance at history would reveal that both organizations have tried to make peace with Israel lots of times. It's the Israeli hypocrisy, and a desire for world domination, harbored secretly by conservatives among Jews and Christians, that prevents Israelis from *actually* honoring their peace agreements with the Arab leaders. Here's a brief breakdown of the failed peace efforts between Israel and the PLO or Hamas:

PLO and Peace Efforts

In the '90s, PLO's goals witnessed a major shift from the total annihilation of Israel to accepting Israel's existence. The fall of the Oslo Accords and the rise of fascists like Netanyahu made PLO disillusioned with any prospects of peace with Israel, however. Similarly, Israelis didn't want to give Palestinians the Right of Return because it would destroy the Jewish nature of the Zionist state. The very fact that Israelis don't want Palestinians back in their homeland shows the hypocrisy of their so-called "peace efforts."

Hamas and Peace Efforts

In 2004, Hamas *actually* angered the Palestinian Islamic Jihad by declaring a ceasefire with Israel. Four years later, Hamas proposed a truce with the Zionist regime in case Israel went back to its 1967 borders and gave Palestinians the Right of Return. In 2010, Ismail Haniyeh even showed his support for peace in case a Palestinian referendum showed that most Palestinians wanted peace with Israel. However, Israel refused to show any interest in any peace initiatives.

What's the Way Forward Now?

> *"I think that, in the Zionist movement, Western Jews have assimilated gentile Western Civilization in the most unfortunate possible form ... The seizure of the houses, lands, and property of the 900,000 Palestinian Arabs who are now refugees is on a moral level with the worst crimes and injustices committed during the last four or five centuries by gentile Western European conquerors and colonists overseas." — Toynbee in A Study of History.*

As the Presidential election in the US comes closer, and the two contenders - Kamala and Trump - become invested in the fight to claim the White House, the Palestinians remain indifferent. Whether you vote for a Republican candidate or a Democratic one, both of them will remain staunch supporters of Israel.

Even Biden has been staunchly pro-Israel his entire life, heavily backed by Israeli donors in the U.S., building his political alliances around this support. Yet, he doesn't see the bigger picture. Globally, the situation is changing rapidly, however. It's becoming apparent that he and European leaders misjudged their decision to engage in the war against Russia. They are losing that war with no signs of reversing the situation. Despite escalating the conflict by sending tanks, land-to-air missiles, and even F-15 fighter planes, their efforts have been futile.

Much of the world is now supporting Hamas. Each act of violence in Gaza only breeds more resistance, as every death inspires new members to join Hamas. This is a self-destructive policy, but many in Israel fail to recognize it. America has miscalculated before, in Iraq and Afghanistan, where the Taliban now reigns. Similarly, the Israeli population, around six to eight million, is not strong enough to take on the entire world. It's a delusion to think they can destroy Hamas, whether militarily or economically. They can't even control Gaza.

Mr. Biden also miscalculated within his own country, believing the U.S. would unanimously support Israel. Surprisingly, many American Jews are now sympathizing with the people of Gaza and the Palestinians. The fact is, the "Israel project" faces significant historical impracticalities. People are slowly realizing that Palestinians were bamboozled by both the US and the Palestinian Authority in the name of peace. The term, "peace," when used by subjugators, is a way to keep you docile and incapable of resisting. Palestinians are now resisting harder than ever, and the days of Zionist tyranny are numbered.

When the genocide of Gazans began in October, under the guise of a mission to eliminate Hamas, many individuals started asking: *What would MLK have thought about this whole issue if he were alive today?* As many readers know, MLK had a soft spot for Israel, and he regarded anti-Zionism as the same thing as antisemitism (Palumbo-Liu, 2019). I remember back in February 2024, I was debating a friend of mine who repeated the same talking points about MLK not being openly critical of Israel. That's when I reminded him that many leading historians have criticized Israel and compared the Zionist treatment of Arabs as just as evil as the Nazi treatment of Jews. I told them that the famous historian, Toynbee, believed that what Israelis did to Arabs was worse (morally, not statistically) than what Nazis did to the Jews and the Jews *actually* never had the right to occupy Palestine, even though they were like a fossil of the ancient people (Ben-Israel, 2006).

My friend agreed with me and confessed that if MLK were alive today, the Gazan Genocide would have *certainly* changed his mind about Israel being a legitimate state. After all, Israel's genocidal campaign in Gaza has influenced Wikipedia editors to such an extent that, after a lengthy debate that lasted weeks (or maybe even months), they decided that Israel was *indeed* conducting a genocide of Gazans (Goichman, 2024). We have examples of former IDF soldiers who went on to study genocides and realized that what their government did to Palestinians was exactly what Germans had done to them in the '30s and '40s (Bartov, 2024). The tide is turning, and the end of Israel is near. Now, it's up to Israelis whether they turn against their government and stage a revolution or keep supporting this genocide, only to be defeated by a powerful alliance of freedom fighters.

In the next chapter, we'll discuss the recent genocidal campaign of Israel in Gaza. What happened on the memorable day of October 7? Why do Israelis call it their 9/11? Was it justified or not? Who *actually* committed those murders? Does 10/7 give Jews the right to collectively punish all Palestinians? We'll give a great response to the usual Zionist arguments and talking points. You'll learn how 10/7 only reveals how Israelis deem Palestinians as less than humans and consider their blood cheaper than water.

11. Current Genocide in Gaza (October 7, 2023 to September 30, 2024)

"You, the people of Palestine, have the right to hold your heads high, as you challenge the world's greatest power. The world is bewildered by the greatness and the secret of the strength of the people of Gaza. **You are blessed with the promise of your Lord***, and the covenant of your Prophet." Abu Obaidah.*

In the heart of Gaza, where chaos reigns and the despair of war casts a huge shadow on every face, the world meets yet another shocking tragedy. Mohamed Abu al-Qumsan had recently become a dad. His wife gave birth to twins Asser and Aysel. Beaming with joy, Mohamed went to register the birth of his children, a moment he had been anticipating for a long time. His heart brimmed with joy and love as he envisioned the future. He and his wife would raise these twins at their modest home in Deir al-Balah, where this family of four had sought refuge since their expulsion from Gaza City. As he stood in the simple government office to register the birth of his newborns, a devastating phone call shattered his whole world. An Israeli missile had struck his home, killing his wife and children. Confused and beyond consolation, Mohamed rushed to see for himself whether his family was alive or not. Holding the birth certificates of his twins in one hand and the other shielding his eyes, he took in the haunting remnants of the place he once called home.

For genocide historians, the killing of Abu al-Qumsan's entire family would just be another death statistic. However, for the young Palestinian father, his ambitions and dreams turned into nightmares. The airstrike that claimed his family wasn't an isolated incident. It's part of a broader tragedy facing Palestinians. This story is one of many examples of how the tyrannical regime of Israel is unleashing the monster of war in Palestine. Israel's actions can be regarded as ethnic cleansing, at the very least (even though evidence suggests that it's genocide). For the liberal media, this is just a war, and the thousands of dead Palestinians are merely "the human cost of conflict." For a person searching for truth, however, it's a deliberate attempt at eradicating Palestine as a nation. The twins of Mohamed Abu al-Qumsan aren't the only individuals who lost their lives to violent Israeli attacks. I can *personally* name people who were killed, just because Israel doesn't care if Gazans live or die. Media has mentioned some names who have died in the Gazan Genocide, such as (Strzyżyńska et al., 2023):

- *Besan Helasa*, a young medical student killed by Israelis along with her two siblings and mother.

- *Saidam al-Shaima*, a brilliant student was killed along with her family in a refugee camp.

- *Yousef M. Dawas*, a poet/writer lost his life in Beit Lahia to Israeli airstrikes.

- *The Shaban's*, a small family of mom, dad, and four young children, was killed by an Israeli missile.

- *Iyad Abdelaziz Asker*, a child killed by Israelis in a refugee camp.

For the West, the dead Palestinians are just names, casualties reflected as statistics, the victims of "a war on Hamas." For us, these are not merely names. These are real people no longer alive because Israel indiscriminately bombs military sites and refugee camps, hospitals, tunnels, militants, and civilians just walking down the street to buy groceries. Israeli soldiers, settlers, and others all have blood on their hands. This mirrors the horrors of al-Nakbah and the Gazan Genocide of 2014.

Israel claims that 10/7 was its 9/11. Palestinians have seen dozens of 10/7s and hundreds of 9/11s. However, the ongoing Gazan Genocide started because Hamas attacked Israelis on October 7, 2023. In retaliation, a tyrannical regime is now murdering Palestinians, punishing them collectively for Hamas's actions. So, let's unpack the background of October Seven. How has 10/7 changed the lives of Gazans forever? What is the evidence that Israel is committing genocide in Gaza? This eye-opening chapter will illustrate that the moral responsibility of Hamas's military campaigns ultimately falls on Israel, the regime forcing Palestinians to live with apartheid.

"Israel's 9/11": A Brief Recount of *Tufan al-Aqsa*ˆ

The Western media calls 10/7 another "escalation in the long-standing Israel-Palestine conflict." This is not merely a "conflict." The extermination of Gazans at the hands of Jews is genocide. Let's review the background of this genocide. Why did it happen? Why did Hamas attack Israel? What was the point of the al-Aqsa Flood/Storm? After all, this military operation involved the launch of thousands of rockets and ground incursions into Israeli territory, resulting in substantial casualties and a rapid response from Israel. Let's dive into the historical context of this event first.

- **The Arab-Israeli War:** The emergence of Israel is the reason behind Hamas's. It led to the displacement of Palestinians and started their seventy-five-year-long suffering, transforming things into an apartheid-like situation.

- **The Six-Day War:** Israel used this war as a pretext by to capture different territories, such as the West Bank and Gaza.

That's why Palestinian militants and peace activists alike have asked Israel to go back to its pre-1967 borders.

- **The Oslo Accords:** This agreement was a great moment for Israel to grant Palestinians their valid rights. However, Israel didn't honor the articles of this agreement, leading to disappointment and mistrust among Palestinians.

- **The Two Intifadas:** The two Intifadas also highlighted the harsh realities of Israeli occupation. It convinced Palestinians that armed resistance was the only way to ensure their well-being. So, Hamas's actions on 10/7 could be described as the Third Intifada.

The Events of 10/7—What Happened?

So, what happened on October 7? On the morning of that fateful day, Hamas launched an attack on Israel, a military campaign historically unprecedented. It was also the holiday of Simchat Torah and Shemini Atzeret. Firing over 5,000 rockets within a very short period marked the first time since the 1948 Arab-Israeli War when a Palestinian military group successfully infiltrated Israeli territory on such a large scale. Reports indicate that the ensuing brawl between Hamas and IDF resulted in the death of 1,200 Israelis—civilians and soldiers alike. Hamas took multiple hostages, and their rescue was used as a pretext to launch a genocidal campaign against Palestinians.

This event is seen as a turning point in the Israeli-Palestinian relationship, reminding us of major events like the Yom Kippur War (1973). The Israeli response reminds us of the 2014 genocide in Gaza committed by a tyrannical regime. The killing of 1,200 Israelis became an excuse for bloodthirsty Zionists to launch a mission to eradicate the population of Gaza. After all, Jewish rabbis have previously proclaimed that a million Arabs weren't worth even a single Jewish fingernail. Let's see how many Palestinians have succumbed to Israel's tyranny as of September 2024.

Military Escalations: 10/7 from a Gazan's Perspective

> *"Now go, attack the Amalekites and totally destroy all that belongs to them. Do not spare them; put to death men and women, children and infants, cattle and sheep, camels and donkeys." — 1 Samuel 15:3.*

Israel conducted numerous airstrikes and ground operations in Gaza. Even though Israel claims that it has only targeted military assets, we can see that not even schools, hospitals, residential apartments, and even refugee camps were spared the wrath of the Israelis. Bible verses were quoted to compare Palestinians with a race called "Amalek," justifying the killing of civilians. Over 100,000 Palestinians are now dead, and more than 85 percent of those who are alive are affected by these airstrikes.

The genocide has also affected the West Bank. Even before Israel decided to invade it in August 2024, West Bank (or, as Israel likes to call it, Judea and Samaria) residents were facing settler attacks. The settler population initiated over 1,200 attacks against Palestinians, leading to over a hundred deaths. In areas like Jenin and Tulkarem, IDF soldiers attacked civilians and inflicted countless casualties. Israeli soldiers are notorious for using women and children for target practice. Even though 2023 was already called the deadliest year for children in Palestine just before October 7, Israel broke its *own* record after 10/7. The genocidal campaign also caused waves in the neighboring countries. Israel's offensive against civilians in the wake of 10/7 activated Hezbollah yet again in this conflict.

Humanitarian Crises: Health, Education, and Living

When talking about the humanitarian crises that followed Israel's invasion of Gaza, we can describe it in many different ways. The Gazan Genocide is a multifaceted topic, and the devastation of Palestine has many aspects, such as well-being, education, and living conditions. Let's break it down for brevity, shall we?

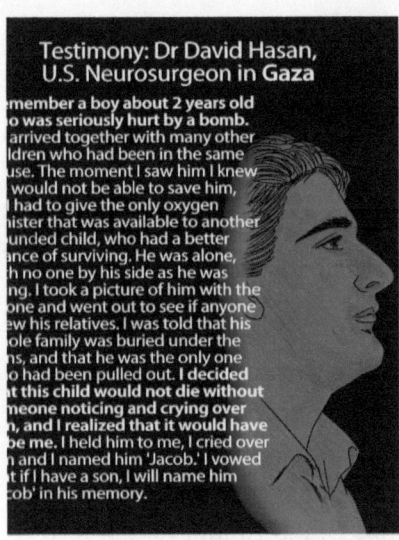

Testimony: Dr David Hasan, U.S. Neurosurgeon in Gaza

...member a boy about 2 years old ...o was seriously hurt by a bomb. ...arrived together with many other ...ldren who had been in the same ...use. The moment I saw him I knew ...would not be able to save him, ...had to give the only oxygen ...ister that was available to another ...unded child, who had a better ...ance of surviving. He was alone, ...h no one by his side as he was ...ng. I took a picture of him with the ...one and went out to see if anyone ...ew his relatives. I was told that his ...ole family was buried under the ...ns, and that he was the only one ...o had been pulled out. **I decided ...t this child would not die without ...meone noticing and crying over ...n, and I realized that it would have ...be me.** I held him to me, I cried over ...n and I named him 'Jacob.' I vowed ...t if I have a son, I will name him ...ob' in his memory.

• **The Health Crisis in Gaza:** Reporters noted that over 12,000 children died in Gaza between October and February; almost 33,000 were injured, while around 25,000 had lost either one parent or both (Brabenec, 2024). Moreover, experts realized that eight out of ten starving persons on Earth were located in Gaza; 25 percent of the population was starving, and one-half of these starving Gazans were children. Similarly, six out of ten structures in Gaza had been flattened, while 86 percent of the residents were displaced from their homes. In May, it was reported that 34,000 Palestinians were dead while 78,000 were wounded. The death count of children increased by 2,000, and seven out of ten buildings were destroyed by Israel (Bouranova, 2024). In August, news agencies revealed that 40,000 Palestinians were dead (the actual number is expected to be much higher). Even though Israel claims that 17,000 of these casualties belonged to militants, we know that Israel has a habit of dressing civilians as militants and then shooting them mercilessly without trial.

• **The Education Crisis:** Israeli airstrikes indiscriminately targeted schools and colleges. As per a report by *Save the Children*, Israel has destroyed or damaged 80 to 90 percent of the school buildings in Gaza. This has led many children to drop out of school (since they can either go to school or survive)—likely the largest pedagogical crisis of this century. The psychological trauma experienced by children due to the conflict has also had a significant impact on their ability to learn and thrive. A joint statement by UNICEF, the World Health Organization, and other UN agencies warned of the terrible consequences of the war on children's mental health, with every child in Palestine having experienced profoundly distressing events and trauma. The story of the Tabaeen School shocked many people when Israel killed over eighty Palestinians and claimed that some of them were militants. A closer look at the list of so-called dead militants provided by the IDF revealed that they had recycled names of long-dead Hamas militants and even depicted harmless civilians as terrorists (Prashad, 2024).

- **The Societal Crisis:** As of this writing, the current living conditions of Palestinians are abysmal. Living under Israel's blockade was already difficult. Now, Gazans don't have homes, drinking water, medical facilities, or even a shelter where they can avoid missile attacks from Israel. Families are forced to hide in overcrowded and unsanitary refugee camps. Reports have stated that a staggering 90 percent drop in electricity was noted in Gaza. These conditions have led to the spread of diseases in refugee camps, transforming them into a "living nightmare." Organizations like Doctors Without Borders, the Red Cross, and various UN agencies have warned of a dire humanitarian collapse with a potential death toll exceeding 186,000 due to the intensity of the conflict and its indirect consequences.

Considering these results of Israel's invasion, the International Court of Justice (ICJ) determined that the accusations of the Gazan Genocide were plausible (Al-Kassab, 2024). However, even those who deny the genocide accusation still have to confess that what Israel is doing to Gazans qualifies as ethnic cleansing. This is a case of Jews committing war crimes against Muslims! In the words of Michael Becker, a teacher of international human rights law in Dublin: "Debates about whether Israel's actions constitute genocide or ethnic cleansing are an unhelpful distraction from the fact that we are witnessing a situation of mass atrocity involving what appear to be egregious violations of international law and that states need to press upon Israel to adopt a radically different approach in responding to the threat posed by Hamas."

Essentially, even if you refuse to label Israel's actions as genocide, at the very least, these actions should be condemned and stopped by the international community (Narea & Samuel, 2023).

Within minutes of the International Court of Justice (ICJ) ordering Israel to halt its assault on Rafah, Israel bombed the city again. Even before the ICJ's decision, senior figures had suggested Israel would not comply. If Israel does not comply, questions will arise about whether arms transfers, primarily by the US and Germany, can be made to a state that is continuing to breach an ICJ order.

"No power on Earth will stop Israel from protecting its citizens and going after Hamas in Gaza," government spokesman Avi Hyman said a day before the order. This statement indicates that Israel is likely to break a direct order from the ICJ by continuing its offensive in the southern Gazan city. Sanctions could be imposed on Israel for non-compliance, but that is unlikely from its main allies—the United States, Germany, and the United Kingdom—making any such move symbolic rather than consequential.

The situation raises the question: what now? The options include the status quo, a two-state solution, a confederation, annexation, or a one-state solution. Focus groups conducted in July 2018 and May 2019 collected detailed opinions from over 270 individuals, including West Bank Palestinians and Gazans. The status quo was preferred by Israeli Jews but strongly disliked by Palestinians. West Bank Palestinians' preferred alternative was the two-state solution, while Gazans ranked a one-state solution slightly above the two-state solution.

There is deep distrust and profound animosity between the two sides. Strong, courageous leadership among Israelis, Palestinians, and the international community is necessary to articulate a desire for a better future. A new Palestinian state would require an army to defend itself, protect its borders, and maintain economic control over its borders. Both Israelis and Palestinians reported distrust of their own leadership and the other side's leadership.

A lesson to Israel—as France, Britain, and other countries have learned—is that marginalizing a group within your population is neither safe nor sensible. Terrorists grow under such conditions. The concept of reckless behavior and policy changes is critical. The United States has repeatedly engaged in such actions, often by putting troops on someone else's land. The notion of not negotiating with terrorists is outdated—it is time to reconsider this stance. The ICJ's order is binding, but the court does not have enforcement powers.

International Response and Calls for Peace

When the Gazan Genocide started, Israel issued leaflets to the residents of this tiny territory with this Qur'anic verse: "*Then the Flood overtook them, while they persisted in wrongdoing.*" (Q. 29:14). It was a sarcastic reference to Hamas' Operation al-Aqsa Flood, using the word *Tufan* (Flood) and using it to mock Palestinians. It was also a not-so-subtle indication that all Palestinians were deserving of collective punishment since Israel, blood-thirsty and crazed with anger, condemned all Gazans for Hamas's actions on October Seven. However, the international community had mixed reactions. Some nations celebrated the massacre of Palestinians, some countries condemned Israel, and others were silent. Let's consider a summary of the international response to Israel's invasion of Gaza.

- **Calls for Ceasefire:** Many countries and international organizations have called for a ceasefire in Gaza. From the Pope and the Secretary-General of the United States to the leaders of Ireland and Spain—they have repeated the demand to end the invasion of Gaza.

- **Geopolitical Divisions:** This genocide has also shown deep geopolitical divisions between many countries. For instance, the US, the UK, France, Germany, etc., have expressed support for Israel. However, countries in the Global South are standing in Gaza's corner. Brazil has criticized Israel, while Bolivia has severed ties with it. Pakistan declared Netanyahu a terrorist. China and N. Korea have come out in condemnation of Israel, too.

- **Legal Action:** Billions of people worldwide are demanding to treat Israel as Russia was treated over Ukraine. It's tragic to witness how Putin was branded a terrorist and warrants for his arrest were issued; however, when Netanyahu spoke to Congress, he was welcomed with applause. While countries like South Africa have taken Israel to the ICJ on accusations of genocide, the West's public approval emboldens Israel in its actions.

- **Struggles for Peace:** The Gazan Genocide has reignited discussions about the viability of a Two-State Solution, with many experts arguing that addressing the root causes of the conflict—such as occupation and settlement expansion—is essential for any lasting peace. The European Union has been urged to take a more active role in promoting peace and holding Israel accountable for its actions. Israel's tyranny has also highlighted the need for a comprehensive approach that includes the voices of Palestinian leadership and civil society in any peace negotiations.

We can see that Israel used 10/7 as a pretext to invade Gaza and massacre Gazans. Many organizations in the world have labeled the Jewish response as genocide. To conclude this chapter, we'll discuss several arguments that prove that Israel is *indeed* committing genocide against Palestinians. You'll see why there's a compelling case against Zionists and how the Palestinian struggle and resistance against an invading force as brutal as Israel is 100 percent justified.

Concluding Remarks: The Ten Stages of Genocide

In the previous ten chapters, we have built a case against Israel, proving how the actions of the Zionist regime in Gaza constitute genocide. In this chapter, we have discussed the events of 10/7 to explain how every genocidal campaign in history always uses excuses like, "We are eradicating terrorists" or "We are merely defending ourselves." However, let's go into more detail here and reflect on the ten stages of genocide, which strengthens the case against Israel. These ten stages are as follows:

1. *Dividing yourself and your victims into "us" and "them."*

2. *Hate speech and symbolizing victims as monsters or animals.*

3. *Discriminating against them by passing hateful laws and policies.*

4. *Dehumanizing them by calling them insects, vermin, or human animals.*

5. *Using organized forces to wage a military campaign against victims.*

6. *Denying them fundamental rights and civil liberties with extreme polarization.*

7. *Preparing for genocide by labeling and identifying victims based on ethnic or religious grounds.*

8. *Using illegal prison sentences, ghettos, forced displacement, extrajudicial killings, concentration camps, etc. to discriminate against victims.*

9. *Exterminating your victim as a final solution to a fictional problem.*

10. *Denying that you even committed genocide against victims or blaming them for their plight.*

Now, let's see some examples of these stages in the words of not random Israelis, not a typical Jew from a nameless street in Hebron, not Reddit users barking untruths about Gazans—but from the horse's mouth, i.e., how top Israeli leaders, politicians, and government have spewed many genocidal statements in the last eleven to twelve months. Here are some examples:

- *"We are fighting against human animals and will act accordingly." (Yoav Gallant)*

- *"All the civilian population in Gaza is ordered to leave immediately. We will win. They will not receive a drop of water or a single battery until they leave the world." (Israel Katz)*

- *"It is not true, this rhetoric about civilians being not aware, not involved." (Isaac Herzog)*

- *"Gaza Strip should be flattened, and for all of them there is but one sentence, and that is death." (Yitzhak Kroizer)*

- *"There will be no electricity and no water [in Gaza]; there will only be destruction. You wanted hell, you will get hell." (Ghassan Alian)*

- *"Creating a severe humanitarian crisis in Gaza is a necessary means to achieving the goal." (Giora Eiland)*

- *"There is one and only solution, which is to completely destroy Gaza before invading it." (Moshe Feiglin)*

In light of all these statements, it should become apparent to you that Israel is committing genocide. The world is watching silently as Israel rids the stolen land of its original inhabitants. However, just as many Americans won't confess that their ancestors exterminated Native Americans, many Zionists won't ever admit that what they're watching right now is a full-blown *Final Solution to the Palestinian Question*. It will take the world a few decades to start condemning Israel. By then, it will be too late … too late!

12. The Two-State Solution

"... the two-state solution is the only way to achieve a just and lasting peace between Israelis and Palestinians. It is the only way to ensure Israel's future as a Jewish and democratic state, living in peace and security with its neighbors. It is the only way to ensure a future of freedom and dignity for the Palestinian people." — John Kerry.

Let's imagine a story: A guy breaks into your home and kicks you out. You and your loved ones are living on the street and have to fight off other homeless people for goods and scraps. Meanwhile, the usurper turns your home into a five-story apartment, inviting their close relatives to live there rent-free. All you can do is watch your former home being inhabited by random strangers who somehow are under the impression that this building is rightfully theirs.

You are determined to do something about it. After all, this house was built a century ago by your great-grandfather, who moved here from Italy with the "shirt on his back and a dollar in his pocket." He spent his life savings erecting this humble yet beautiful abode for his offspring. Now, you're forced to watch others living in this house while your kids are starving. You go to the cops for help and show them your papers. These papers show that this house is yours. What do the cops do? They suggest dividing it between you and the usurpers. Don't you think it's a grave act of injustice to ask legal homeowners to share their homes with outsiders who have no right to occupy your property?

That's the story of Israel and Palestine, a story of the battle between occupants and true homeowners. So, it's no surprise that the Two-State Solution isn't something most Palestinians find appealing. A poll from 2021 shows that less than 40 percent of Palestinians accept the idea of a Two-State Solution, while almost six out of ten Palestinians reject it altogether (Public Poll Opinion, 2021). For many, arguing for this solution is as preposterous as arguing for apartheid in South Africa or arguing for peace between Jews and Nazis. What are our arguments against the Two-State Solution? What is the alternative to it? We'll address it all in the next few sections of this chapter.

Submission or Friendship: The Two-State Solution

On the historic date of Nov 29, 2012, the UN General Assembly recognized Palestine as an observer state. This decision was supported by 138 countries. Nine countries voted against it, while forty-six were absent. The very next day, Netanyahu announced the construction of thousands of new settlements in the E-1 area. Several nations tried to convince the Israelis not to build these settlements. But their efforts were fruitless. This is the truth behind the Two-State Solution: it's akin to begging a lion who kills four of your cubs every week to kill only two. The lion promises to refrain from killing two but ends up snatching five the very next week. You don't tame the lion. You cut its paws off!

However, many Western countries and Arab nations want Palestinians to befriend the lion and live with it from now on. They propose something called the Two-State Solution, a framework aimed at resolving the Israeli-Palestinian rivalry—if that's how you can describe the relationship between Hebrews and Nazis as well—by creating two independent states: Israel (for Jews) and Palestine (for Arabs).

Historical Background and Key Components

The roots of this solution go back many decades. It's not a novel solution, nor a unique idea. If you are diligent enough, you can find many instances in human history where the same solution was utilized to bring peace between two conflicting nations, e.g., the two Koreas, the two Germanys, the splitting of Sudan, India, and Pakistan, East Timor separating from Indonesia, the American Civil War, etc.

In the case of Israel and Palestine, the UN proposed a partition plan (Resolution 181) to create two states for Jews and Arabs, respectively. However, the event of al-Nakbah prevented this plan from becoming an impressionable reality. Jews won a state of their own, while Palestinians were left stranded and expelled from their homeland by the victorious Hebrews.

The Oslo Accords breathed new life into the idea of two states in Palestine. For the first time in history, a Jewish Prime Minister of Israel agreed to a semblance of an independent state for the people of Palestine. However, the Israeli establishment has no intention of actually giving Palestinians a state of their own. Instead, the Palestinian Authority (PA) backstabbed the people they were supposed to serve! A Ramallah-based government started working with Israelis, driven by self-interest. The weakness of the PA, as a result, was the final nail in the coffin of the proposed Two-State Solution. If it were realized, the states formed in the region followed these key components:

- **Territorial Division**: We would get a Palestinian state composed of parts from the West Bank and the Gaza Strip. The borders of this state would be based on pre-1967 lines, subject to mutually agreed land swaps to accommodate Israeli settlements.

- **The Status of Jerusalem**: East Jerusalem would serve as the capital of a future Palestinian state, while West Jerusalem would remain Israel's capital. As a result, both states would share the city and its administrative control.

- **Security Arrangements**: Both states would ensure security for citizens, such as demilitarizing the Palestinian state and cooperation in counter-terrorism efforts. However, this condition was included just to let Israel attack Palestine whenever it desired.

- **Recognition and Sovereignty**: The solution requires mutual recognition of both states' right to exist. The PLO recognized Israel's right to exist since the Accords, while Israel has been urged to recognize Palestinian aspirations for statehood.

When Trump recognized Jerusalem as the capital of Israel, it proved once and for all that the US government was never serious about creating a Palestinian state. The Deep State of America was always colluding with Israel, fighting for its right to prevent the formation of a Palestinian state in the future. The actions of Trump weren't a reflection of his poor judgment or closeness with Israelis; it was a reflection of the deeply rooted hatred for third-world countries in the US government's mind. On the other hand, Netanyahu and his likes have always worked against the independence of Palestinians. The Butcher of Gaza has repeatedly voiced his opinion on this issue:

1. **Two States:** He said in 2015 that there would be no Palestinian country as long as he's the PM of Israel (Azulay, 2015).

2. **One State:** He is even against the One-State Solution, i.e., the idea of turning Israel into a secular nation where Jews and non-Jews are equal (Salem & Salem, 2024).

However, the world has only heard the arguments of Zionists about how the Two-State Solution is futile. Now, we'll consider the arguments against this solution from the Palestinian side. What do Palestinians say about the Two-State Solution? Why do so many Gazans disapprove of this proposal? What is the planned alternative to the Two-State Solution? Let's look into it in the next section.

Arguments against the Two-State Solution: From a Palestinian's Perspective

You may think that my Palestinian heritage is the reason I'm against the Two-State Solution. Here, I shall first show you what the experts in Middle Eastern studies have to say on this topic. In 2021, Biden said that he would listen to academics on the "Israel-Palestine Conflict."

As a result, academics who were experts in Arab studies shared their findings with him. Fifty-two percent of experts believed that the likelihood of the Two-State Solution materializing had decreased below the point of credulity. Here is what they were thinking would happen to the people of Palestine if the Two-State Solution didn't succeed (Lynch & Telhami, 2021):

- 77 percent of them predicted there would be apartheid

- 17 percent of them predicted inequalities would increase without apartheid

- 1 percent of them predicted Palestinians would receive equal rights in Israel

Even the PLO realized back in 2014 that the Two-State Solution existed "in name only." Erekat, the PLO's Secretary General, openly said that the Israeli government was burying the idea of a Palestinian state. They wanted to barter Palestinian statehood with a two-tier apartheid system. So, why don't Palestinians want to follow the carrot of the Two-State Solution anymore? In my opinion, here are some major arguments in favor of the utter and complete failure of this solution:

5-Reasons the Two-State Solution is Not Viable

1. **Imbalance of Power:** The asymmetry of power/influence between Israel and Palestine is a major reason the formation of two states won't work the way Palestinians want. Israel is stronger regarding military power, global influence, economic virility, diplomatic advantages, and tech. It's the same imbalance of power that allowed the Nazis to take over Europe. So, any agreement reached under such conditions would likely be inequitable and unsustainable.

2. **Silent Expansion:** As Israel plans to expand its genocide into southern Lebanon, it keeps raising more illegal settlements in the West Bank. This expansion means that Israel won't stay

idle even after a Palestinian state is created. The existence of Israel is an existential threat to Palestinians. A survey shows that over 650,000 illegal settlers inhabit the West Bank and East Jerusalem.

3. **Historical Precedents:** Many people forget that Jews and Arabs lived side by side before 1948. Then, the al-Nakbah happened, and the Palestinians were kicked out of their homeland. How do we know that Israel won't do the same to the Palestinians after we get a new state? The potential for interethnic violence during a transition phase raises concerns about the stability and safety of both communities.

4. **No Political Will:** The PA is in bed with Israel and not interested in the well-being of Gazans. On the other hand, Israel has repeatedly shown its ambition to either massacre all Palestinians or push them out of Palestine forever. With the right-wing Zionist blocks dominant in the Knesset, there is no chance that a Two-State Solution would materialize anytime soon.

5. **No Better Alternatives:** Politicians have failed to propose better alternatives to the Two-State Solution (or, let's say, they are not interested in figuring one out). The most popular alternative is the One-State Solution. However, most Israelis oppose this solution. It would make Israel normal, and normalcy is what Zionists can't tolerate due to their bloodthirsty nature. The fixed national identities and historical grievances make coexistence within a single state fraught with difficulties. Critics argue that without addressing these deep-seated issues, any solution—whether two states or one—will likely lead to ongoing conflict rather than resolution.

Pros and Cons of the Two-State Solution

In short, here are the pros and cons of this solution from a neutral perspective:

Pros	Cons
The international community is overwhelmingly in favor of Palestinian statehood. More than two-thirds of the members of the UN want a two-state solution to this problem.	No significant progress has been made toward this solution since the Oslo Accords. Experts believe that now, only a small group of Israelis are in favor of the Two-State Solution. Most Israelis are very strict in their Zionism and want only the supremacy of Israel, "from the River to the Sea."
Most Jews want to keep the Jewish identity of their country, so the Two-State Solution allows them to keep Israel a Jewish-first nation.	Zionists are establishing illegal settlements in the Occupied Territories without any shame. It doesn't seem that these illegal occupiers want to share even an inch of this land with the Palestinians.
Integrating Palestine into Israel to create a unified country will alter the socioeconomic demographics of the Zionist nation, putting the burden of care of the poor Palestinian population on the wealthy Israeli government.	It's feared that the presence of two states will only result in Israel trying to dominate the Palestinian state. As a result, there should be more than two states in the region.

A Unique Solution: Creating Three States in the Region

Normally, the term "Three-State Solution" is used for a framework where Egypt controls Gaza, and the governance of the West Bank reverts to Jordan. This is what the proponents of this ludicrous and hypocrisy-fraught proposal imagine would happen: *"If neighboring Jordan, which has been at peace with Israel since 1994, is involved in a peace settlement, Israel will be able to transfer all Palestinian territory to a future Palestinian-Jordanian Federation. This grants Palestinians the right to self-determination within their own state. But as military control over Palestinian territory passes to the federal government in Amman, friendly Jordan will be able to guarantee Israel's security sufficiently to make peace possible* (Tulner, 2024)."

This isn't what I mean when I use the term "Three-State Solution." Gaza shouldn't go to Egypt. It's only a Zionist ploy to make Gazans identify as Egyptians, denying their unalienable right to their homeland in Palestine. Egyptians and Jordanians are Muslim brothers of Palestinians. However, Gazans deserve to live in their separate country, i.e., the Gaza Strip, and rule it. If the whole world favors the Two-State Solution with all its heart, I say: *Why not simply put a third state in the midst?*

What I propose is the formation of three separate states in the region, i.e., Israel, Gaza, and the West Bank. The West Bank is already under the governance of the PA. Gaza would become a separate country. If you think it won't work, please consider the following:

Eight Arguments in Favor of the Three-State Solution

1. **Different Government Structures:** The PA governs the West Bank, while Hamas controls Gaza. As we have seen in the past chapters, these two entities have different political ideologies, governance styles, and long-term goals. They also operate differently. We should acknowledge these differences by letting Gaza and WB become two separate states alongside Israel.

2. **Historical Context:** Historically, Jordan has administered the West Bank, while Gaza was under Egypt's control and influence. So, this historical precedent suggests that separate governance is a feasible option to restore a sense of stability that has been elusive under the PA's rule.

3. **Israel's Interests:** Don't worry, I also have something Israelis would approve of in this proposal. With Gaza and the West Bank as two separate states, Israel's security would improve due to clearer borders and easier relationship management.

Israel could negotiate different security arrangements with the PA and deal with Hamas less diplomatically.

4. **Fewer Chances of Conflict:** Also, the recognition of Gaza as a separate entity would mitigate all or most political tensions that stem from the distinct political agendas of the PA and Hamas. This separation could lead to focused conflict resolution strategies to address the unique challenges of each area (i.e., Gaza and the West Bank) without conflating them into a single narrative.

5. **Tailored Economic Policies:** We shouldn't forget that Gaza and the West Bank have different economic and social conditions, as well. So, the Three-State Solution would let both to develop advantageous economic policies suited to their unique circumstances. For instance, Gaza could benefit from Egyptian support and investment to rebuild its infrastructure, while the West Bank could pursue partnerships with Jordan or even Israel and other nations.

6. **International Support & Investments:** With Gaza as a separate state, it could receive much more international support and investment than as an area under the PA's rule. That's because activists are slowly opening their eyes to the backstabbing nature of Ramallah and realizing how the PA merely colluded with Israel instead of working toward the betterment of the Palestinian people.

7. **Recognizing Current Realities:** The ongoing conflict has created a situation where both territories function almost independently. A three-state solution would formally recognize this reality, allowing for more pragmatic approaches to governance and conflict resolution rather than forcing an unrealistic unification.

8. **Peaceful Coexistence Possible:** Lastly, creating three states in the region will open up many opportunities for peaceful

coexistence among Jews, Muslims, and Christians. Once these groups recognize each other's sovereignty, every entity could negotiate its separate treaties with the Zionist regime. It would foster an environment where cooperation would be prioritized.

The Two-State Mirage: Crushed by Bigotry, Betrayal, and Deception

Hamas was created because of Israel's continuation of occupation, expansion of the settlement, and creation of a Palestinian authority that will be a security agent to suppress the people's resistance. The concession that Fatah gave in Oslo and, for thirty years, gave everyone more excuses for not recognizing Palestinian rights until we reached the current stage of condemning every resistance act and an excuse for all the press to normalize them, considering that Palestinians are in the throes of genocide.

I'm glad the Israelis voted to reject the two-state solution, so we don't have to play this stupid game anymore where we pretend Israelis are serious people who respect diplomacy. They never wanted a Palestinian state. And frankly, what they want is irrelevant! It's not their land, so their opinion doesn't matter. It's like US politicians trying to decide where Native Americans should live.

As the dust settles on yet another failed peace effort, the harsh truth becomes undeniable, i.e., the "Two-State Solution" is nothing more than an illusion, buried under a stinking pile of Israeli bigotry, American betrayal, and the staggering failures of the Palestinian Authority. Israel and its Western allies have made their intentions painfully clear. Their goal has never been peace but rather the complete eradication of the Palestinian cause. Beneath the guise of diplomacy, they tried not only to destroy the dream of an independent Palestine but to also obliterate its people, wielding military power and political scheming without a trace of morality.

The charade of negotiations has collapsed, exposing a ruthless agenda to silence an entire nation. The gullible Arafat was deceived when he hurried to Oslo—he himself acknowledged this in 2001 after Ariel Sharon's provocative entry into *Masjid al-Aqsa* ignited the Second Intifada. The Israeli proposal is clear from these snippets:

1. Likud's original charter and revised charter reject a Palestinian state west of the Jordan River, advocating for exclusive Israeli sovereignty between the Sea and Jordan.

2. The Israeli government asserts the Jewish people's exclusive right to all parts of the Land of Israel.

3. Ben Gurion's plan aimed to expand Israeli territory to all of Palestine after establishing a large army.

When discussing 240 Israeli hostages, we must be prepared to talk about 10,000 Palestinian prisoners as well, including children taken by Israel. Israel is bombing its hostages and refusing their release, so they don't give Hamas another chance to film the releasing of hostages, refute the Israeli narrative, and show the world that hostages are treated humanely, as per the hostages themselves! Talking about violence on 10/7 should include Israeli occupation and a history of violence for seventy-five years. You don't get to decide where the timeline begins (see Chapter Fourteen to realize when it *actually* began).

Despite seventy-five years of occupation, countless UN violations, and several counts of abuses, including torture, rape, murder, and land theft, the focus of the corrupt Western media remains fixed on the Palestinian resistance! Indigenous people who courageously oppose these injustices find themselves labeled as "terrorists," echoing historical events. When Native Americans resisted, they were branded as "savages." Enslaved Africans were dehumanized. Today, Palestinians are branded as terrorists simply for defending their rights.

Israeli war criminals are cutting off essential services in Gaza, including water, food, internet, and electricity, while destroying hospitals, churches, and schools. It's wrong to call this genocide a conflict. With over 30,000 deaths and countless more trapped under the rubble, Gaza's two million residents, mostly women and children, are enduring genocide.

If Israel wants to be a genuine peace partner, it must dismantle its Zionist ideology that deems non-Jews unworthy of the Holy Land. This, including equal respect for Palestinian rights, must be addressed. Then, Hamas would change its charter to acknowledge Israel. Until then, I see no difference between Nelson Mandela's resistance and Hamas's.

If your land was taken and your family killed, you would resist violently, just as any Palestinian, Iraqi, or Afghani would against foreign invaders. I support the right of self-defense and won't condemn it. That's because it strikes a chord with Latin American countries, who have been victims of European colonialism and American imperialism. But it is also important to mention that Brazil supported the Palestinian cause even during the long military dictatorship (1964-1985) and has supported a two-state solution, a position that Lula also pushed forward as he became president in 2003.

13. The Palestinian Dream and Future Hopes

"And what is [the matter] with you that you fight not in the cause of Allah and [for] the oppressed among men, women, and children who say, "Our Lord, take us out of this city of oppressive people and appoint for us from Yourself a protector and appoint for us from Yourself a helper?" — (Q. 4:75).

Shortly before his death, the great Palestinian author and researcher Edward Said gave an interview on the the Israel-Palestine issue. He was asked if Zionists had a valid claim on Palestine. The scholarly yet subtle professor responded to this question beautifully. He said that the Jewish claim isn't the only claim. It's a "claim among many others. "Biblical archeologists believe that Jews have maintained (regarding the Old Testament) a historic presence for two to three centuries in Palestine. Other nations, such as the Jebusites, Canaanites, and Philistines, have also maintained a presence in Palestine. It must be noted, however, that "Arabs have a much greater claim because they have had a longer history of inhabitants." In Said's eloquent words, it's utterly irrational for a Jew from Poland or Brooklyn to tell the Arab residents of Palestine to get out of their homes (Canada Talks Israel/Palestine, 2017).

You may have seen videos circulating online of people who were kicked out of their homes in the events of al-Nakbah. Now, they come back to find their ancestral homes occupied by Jews from Eastern Europe, claiming that God had granted them the right to conquer this territory. If that isn't fundamentalism, what do you call it then? Zionism is the only form of religious extremism that's acceptable in the West—the only form of extremism tolerated by Americans and Europeans. But the tide is changing, and the world is waking up to realize that Zionism has to go. It has no place in an age where secularism and liberalism rule the world. In the words of Riyad Mansour, "The Palestinian people will be free one day or another, one way or another." We can practically imagine a future where Palestine achieves freedom, and the occupation ends. A new future begins for the Arabs who were expelled by Jews from Palestine. The refugees are allowed to return, and children can play without having to constantly worry about Israeli airstrikes. If you asked me to paint a picture of this future, it'd be something like this:

Little Fatima gazes out over the sun-kissed beaches of Gaza as a gentle breeze caresses her face. She recalls the days of the occupation when she was haunted by the stomping of the approaching steps of Zionist troops. However, her family had always remained hopeful that one day, they would walk their ancestral lands without fear. Now, this dream has been realized, and the phoenix of Palestinian resilience is raised from the ashes of al-Nakbah. Fatima smiles as she watches her siblings play on the shores of the motherland. Their laughter echoes across the waves. No more having to navigate intimidating checkpoints or fearing the presence of armed soldiers for her family! Her father, Nabil, strolls past Ramallah's busy markets alive with the scent of spices, the lively chatter of reunited neighbors, and the music of outbound airplanes returning settlers to their countries of origin while Palestinian Airlines welcome passengers to their homeland. The refugees of the past will now become the nation's new residents.

These scattered migrants have been roaming the globe ever since the Zionists banished their ancestors. They can now settle in their homeland after a hundred years, able to bow down in Mecca's direction and place their foreheads humbly on the soil that nourished their forefathers in the days of the Ottoman Empire. The days of occupation spanned ten decades, but now Palestinians can replace their trauma with healing. In Gaza, families are no longer dispersing across different locations for protection or sleeping in different rooms in case an airstrike in the dead of night turns them from living, breathing human beings into statistics for a genocide historian's research. They realize that their homes will no longer be reduced to rubble by Israel under the pretext of "hunting down Hamas." Mothers don't have to label their children's bodies now. The specters of war and apartheid are banished. Palestinians can now face a future of peace and prosperity face.

As the sun dips below the horizon, casting a warm glow over the land, Fatima and Nabil join hands, their eyes shining with tears of joy and pride. They are home, and they are free. The Palestinian dream has now become a reality, and it's a dream that will continue to inspire generations to come. As the evening looms, Nabil buries the coffin bearing his grandfather's remains. The old man wanted to do what Joseph had done and asked for his body to be buried in his ancestral village when Palestinians were allowed to return to their motherland. Now, Nabil has fulfilled the old man's last wishes. His grandfather left the village as a refugee, forced to flee to save his life. But he's now buried next to his ancestors, sleeping like a man who is finally free!

Voices of Resilience and Determination in Gaza

I remember how, in the early days of the Gaza Genocide, some Zionists on X (formerly Twitter) made fun of Palestinians by uttering pathetic remarks like, "Don't start a war you can't finish," and "Just return the hostages, and it'll be all over." Now, we know that Netanyahu has proclaimed that he'll continue bombing Gaza even if Hamas agrees to a ceasefire and frees the hostages (VOA News, 2024). These remarks hurt me deeply as I observed how Zionists dehumanized my people and trivialized their suffering. They blamed Gazans for their *own* suffering. I started gathering study materials to write this book immediately. Propping up my laptop, I googled news on the death of Palestinian kids. One of the very first links was from 2022, discussing the deaths of sixteen Palestinian children killed by Israel. I realized that the Gazan Genocide was already in motion before October Seven.

From Muhammad al-Durrah to Faris Odeh to Khalil al-Mughrabi to Salah Shehad—the list goes on! A war on Gaza is *essentially* a war on innocent children. Tears flowed as I read that a child under six was shot in the head every two weeks during the events of the First Intifada. What is even sadder is that Israel's war on children has intensified since October Seven. Every fifteen minutes, a child dies at the hands of Israel in Palestine. And it's not only Israeli soldiers killing them—settlers have also become some of the worst enemies of Palestinian children, killing three dozen in 2024 alone (Obeidat, 2024)! The war in Gaza has taken a devastating toll on the lives of many Palestinians, shattering their hopes and dreams before they even had a chance to take flight. Among the victims are children whose futures have been cruelly cut short by the violence. Some of these kids wanted to:

- Become doctors so they could heal the wounds of war-torn Gazans, but their lives were cut short by Israel's incessant bombing.

- Play soccer in the narrow streets of Rafah, with the desire to represent Palestine on the world stage one day, but their dreams died with them when an Israeli shell struck near their school.

- Travel the world, see what life is like outside of Palestine, and make friends in other nations. But Israel robbed them of this dream when an IDF soldier shot them, accusing them of being adult fighters.

- Excelling in their studies so they could break free from this cycle of poverty and violence that defined their childhood in Khan Younis, but losing their family to Zionist airstrikes made it impossible to focus on their education.

It all happened because Jews from Eastern Europe wanted compensation for the Holocaust, but the leaders of Europe decided to give them a piece of land in the Middle East. Palestinians paid the price for the sins of the White man! The "White Man's Burden" ultimately revealed itself to be a form of *kappator*, a ritual in which Orthodox Jews pass their sins to a chicken and then slaughter it. In this case, Palestinians were chosen by Zionists to pay for the crimes of Europeans. The prophet Isaiah had already predicted this when he uttered these words:

> *"Ah, sinful nation, a people loaded down with wickedness, offspring of evildoers, sons who behave corruptly! They have abandoned the Lord ... They have turned away from Him ... You continue to rebel. The whole head is sick, and the whole heart is faint and sick." — (Isaiah 1:4-5).*

However, even though Zionists have abandoned the Lord and turned away from Him, Palestinians are still standing strong, hoping for His mercy and victory in the end. You'll hear the hum of resilience, courage, and determination coming out of Gaza, but only if you disregard the noise of Jewish propaganda. The indomitable spirit of the people of Palestine makes a Zionist tremble in fear. We can recount many stories of Gazans—sons and daughters of the soil—who are standing firm in the face of Zionist oppression. Some of these brave children of Gaza are:

- **Hala:** This forty-seven-year-old woman became a symbol of resilience when she was forced to escape her humble abode in Al Bureij. Seeking refuge in a UNRWA school, she was rejected and left there to rest outside while leaning her back against the school wall. But Hala made herself useful by providing psychological support to other women and their children. Being a single mother of four, she has become a beacon of hope as she listens to women's struggles and organizes comfort activities to spread positivity in an otherwise war-torn city (Voices From Gaza, 2023).

- **Ibtisam:** This paraplegic woman is nearly fifty but still filled with hope. Fleeing her house in the suburbs of Bani Suheila, she found a dilapidated shelter at the Red Cross. She lacked a bed made for people with disabilities but realized that she could make this place better by cooking for others. Now, she prepares meals for the Red Cross staff and proves that Gazans haven't lost their willpower. They are ready to take on any challenges that may come their way. Israel may kill their bodies, but their spirits shall live forever on the lands of their forefathers.

- **Journalists:** Amidst the rubble and grief, brave Gazan journalists have emerged as heroes in this genocide. They navigate dangerous conditions to document the harsh realities of life under siege. We have the tales of twenty-two-year-old Plestia Alaqad and others who risk their lives to report on an oppressed Gazan community's daily struggles. These reporters and journalists embody the spirit of resilience of the people of Gaza. Despite the dangers they face, these journalists continue to tell the stories of their people, ensuring that the world hears their voices and understands their plight (Voices of Resilience, 2024).

These stories give us hope, and these brave individuals make us realize that Palestine will be free soon. A Zionist can try their hardest to suppress resistance in the United States, pass laws banning solidarity in the EU, force the UN to do nothing as Israel keeps bombing Palestine, and turn Gaza into *a parking lot*—an outcome many Jews actively wish for—the Palestinian dream shall never end.

Dreams of a Free Palestine and Marwan Barghouthi

> *"I dream of a time when a Palestinian airline proudly welcomes passengers to Palestine. I dream of Palestinian refugees scattered across the globe returning to their homeland, uniting under the shared sky of a unified nation. My neighbors will be Palestinian refugees, each bearing their own unique Arabic accents or perhaps speaking languages like Spanish. In unity, they will rebuild their lives."* — A Nameless Palestinian.

The people of Palestine have always dreamt of a future where they can live in freedom, a future where the occupiers from Europe don't occupy their ancestral lands. While Zionists keep portraying the Palestinian Right of Return as anti-Semitic, it's *actually* a very rational demand of a people unjustly expelled from their homeland. For many Palestinians, the dream of returning to their ancestral homes remains a driving force. Scattered across the globe as refugees, they yearn for the day they can reunite under the flag of a free and independent Palestine.

This vision extends beyond the physical return to a longing for the restoration of a collective identity, where the trauma and PTSD that have haunted the people can finally heal, and they can embrace a future of justice, equality, and self-determination. That's why they follow leaders who help them turn this dream into a reality. These leaders, even when they languish in Israeli prisons, keep the hope alive! These leaders— whether they are peace activists or militants—are the flag bearers of the Palestinian dream.

A Brief Introduction to Marwan Barghouthi

> *"I am against killing innocents. But I am proud of the resistance to Israeli occupation. To die is better than living under occupation." — Marwan Barghouthi.*

We introduced this fellow when talking about PNI's co-founder, Dr. Mustafa Barghouthi. Now, this bloke, Marwan, happens to be Dr. Mustafa's cousin, a symbol of resistance and determination. Born in 1959 in a small village called Kobar, near Ramallah, Barghouthi grew up politically charged from his childhood. He joined Fatah in his teenage years and was arrested by Israel for the first time before his eighteenth birthday.

After spending four years in jail, Marwan Barghouthi had completed his secondary education and learned impressive Hebrew. It would later help him become more politically active in the Occupied Territories. A young Marwan enrolled in Birzeit University to earn a BA in Political

Science, and then did his MA in International Relations. When the First Intifada broke out, Barghouthi was in his twenties. He became one of the key leaders of the Uprising. Even during the Second Intifada, he earned acclaim for his key role as an organizer of protests. Marwan was an excellent advocate for Palestinian rights. It's said that his service helped bridge the gap between Hamas and Fatah.

However, Marwan Barghouthi was arrested in 2002 in Ramallah and convicted in 2004 on charges that weren't adequately proven. It was a typical kangaroo court, where Zionists conspired to imprison the only guy who could unify Palestinians and usher in the era of a true revolution. Despite the Zionist tactics and his imprisonment, Barghouthi remained popular. He's so popular that even his enemies are forced to admit that Marwan's life story eerily parallels the biography of Mandela (Lamb, 2024). This man is so influential that 2012 polls showed that he defeated the likes of Ismail Haniyeh and even the PA's Mahmoud Abbas in popularity (Issacharoff, 2012).

Since 10/7, Marwan has been in solitary confinement, a victim of repeated torture by Zionist guards. However, a man like Barghouthi doesn't easily crumble under pressure. He gives Palestinians hope and keeps them from losing their will to fight. The likes of Marwan Barghouthi also make the international community sympathetic to the cause of Palestine.

Calls for Global Solidarity and Actions for Justice in Gaza and Beyond

About a month ago, I read a piece from Harvard quoting the famous Zionist author, Einat Wilf, who penned a book against the Right of Return, calling it a thinly veiled demand for the destruction of Israel. In that interview, Wilf said that Palestinians had to "abandon an ideology that rejects the legitimacy of a sovereign Jewish state." I almost choked on my tea while reading that. Do Palestinians accept the legitimacy of Israel? An apartheid regime that persecutes them?! That treats them legally as second-class citizens?! No, my dear Wilf! It is Israel that needs to abandon an ideology that discriminates against Arabs and deems their blood cheaper than Jewish blood.

On the other hand, my heart fills with joy when I read statements from Pedro Sánchez, the Spanish Prime Minister, who recently came out in favor of a Palestinian state. More and more countries are learning that Palestinians have always been right about Israel being a genocidal regime. They are now standing with us. In recent months, there's been a notable increase in demonstrations and events advocating for Palestinian rights, particularly in Western cities. These gatherings, fueled by grassroots movements and social media, have united people from diverse backgrounds in a shared commitment to justice.

The visibility of these protests plays a crucial role in raising awareness about the plight of Palestinians, drawing parallels to historical struggles against colonialism and oppression. The rise of global solidarity is evident in these shapes and forms:

- **Remembrance and Protest:** Many countries saw a surge in protests and demonstrations for the victims of Gaza. In the Netherlands, they showcased children's shoes to honor the thousands of kids who were murdered by Israel, emphasizing that these weren't just victims but human beings with names and identities. Similarly, Jewish Voices for Peace organized sit-ins and rallies, calling for a ceasefire. These actions highlight the moral imperative to stand against injustice, echoing sentiments of "never again for anyone."

- **Diaspora Communities Online:** While the likes of DJ Khaled are condemned for keeping mum over the death of their countrymen, we have Bella Hadid being open about the crimes of Israel. In this regard, social media has helped everyday Palestinians—from the ones living in Gaza to those living outside of Gaza—globalize their protest. Diaspora communities play a key role in fighting for their homeland online. They leverage their positions in host countries to raise awareness, lobby governments, and organize solidarity movements for the sake of liberation.

- **Taking Legal Actions:** In the UK, we saw human rights organizations knocking at the front gates of the law to stop the British government from providing weapons to Israel. They argue that these exports defy international humanitarian law. Countries like South Africa and Nicaragua have pursued legal cases against Israel, highlighting the growing international recognition of the need for accountability.

- **Calls for Justice and Peace:** As the reports of starvation and widespread destruction have come out of Gaza—showcasing that this tiny strip of land has become uninhabitable—the ICJ and the UN Human Rights Council have raised concerns regarding Israel's genocide. Many activists also say that the struggle for a free Palestine is intertwined with a broader issue of justice and human rights. Also, activists draw connections between the Palestinian cause and the struggles of indigenous peoples, as well as marginalized communities worldwide, reinforcing the idea that the battle for justice is a shared endeavor.

Shlomo Ben-Ami writes: *"The Palestinians' Second Intifada was a page from the classical theory of anti-colonial revolutionary struggle. It was written into the genetic code of the Palestinian movement of national liberation that, as soon as it became apparent that diplomacy had not produced results, the resort to armed struggle would be a natural option."* That's how he explains the famous slogan that came from the Second Intifada: With Our Soul and Blood, We'll Redeem Palestine (Ben-Ami, 2022). As Israel keeps pushing deeper into this war and continues its genocidal spree, the mask is lifting. The world can see a monster hiding behind the garb of Judaism. God willing, soon this mask shall fall, and the moment it hits the ground, the world shall recognize the Second Coming of Nazism in the clothes of Zionism. Then, the world shall help Palestinians win their freedom!

Final Thoughts on the Palestinian Dream

"Can two walk together, except they are agreed?"
— (Amos 3:3).

Poet Mahmoud Darwish never forgot the moment he was allowed to return to his ancestral home in Palestine after two and a half decades. He described this short visit in this way: "I touched the trees and the stones and felt as if I hadn't left. Time had stopped, and the circle was closed." Darwish was just one of the lucky few who were given the "honor" by the brutal Israeli regime to pay homage to their ancestors and motherland. Unlike Darwish, however, not every Palestinian has a pleasant memory of these visits. In the case of Muhammad 'Ali Taha, he looked for the apricot tree from his childhood. It had disappeared. In other cases, the Jews who occupied houses, not their own, complained that these Arab visitors' constant wailing and mourning disturbed them. Cops came and took the visitors away from their ancestral homes. Imagine the audacity to seize someone else's home and then complain about the victim's tears! That's why many Palestinians who were given a chance to step into their forefathers' homes simply refused to do so. They didn't want to enter their homes as mere visitors. The absurdity of the occupation is illustrated by the many Palestinian villages located just outside the ones they fled from during al-Nakbah—these poor Arab villagers can literally watch from afar as Zionist pillagers live in their homes (Sa'di, 2002).

In the face of ongoing suffering, the dream of a free Palestine rings true! As we reflect on the aspirations of a nation as brave and resilient as Palestine, we are reminded of Nelson Mandela's powerful words: "To deny people their human rights is to challenge their very humanity." Desmond Tutu stated, "It means a great deal to those who are oppressed to know that they are not alone." Today, Gazans know that they have allies all over the world. The struggle for a free Palestine is not isolated. It is *actually* part of a broader fight against injustice that demands our collective action and commitment.

As we envision a day when peace prevails, we hold onto what Ali Abu Awwad has expressed as his firm belief: "The role of nonviolence is to speak to people's despair ... to show them a way out." This path of nonviolence and resilience is essential in the pursuit of lasting peace.

Ultimately, you should know that the dreams of a free Palestine are not merely aspirations but a call to action. Today, as we stand in solidarity with the Palestinian people, we echo the hopes of those who dare to dream of a future where justice, equality, and peace are not just distant ideals but a lived reality. Together, we can work towards a world where the apartheid walls crumble, and the laughter of children fills the air—where Palestinians can finally live in peace, free from fear and oppression.

14. Timeline of the Events from October 2023 to September 2024

"According to the Israeli narrative, nothing, apart from bestial hate, explains October 7, and October 7 justifies everything the Israelis have done since."
— Jewish Voice for Labour.

"History didn't begin on October 7," retorted every pro-Palestinian activist conversing online with Zionists. Many Zionists and their blind supporters require constant reminders that October 7 didn't happen in a vacuum. It's not like Palestinians in Gaza simply hated their Jewish oppressors and one day randomly made up their minds to exterminate Israel. "October 7 has been seventy-five years in the making," says the famous researcher Hussein Ibish (Gridwork, 2023). In 2001, he wrote about the "real question" in Palestine and brought to life the "elephant into the living room of Israeli and American discourse on this conflict." It was the brutal Israeli occupation of the homeland of Gazans. The words of Ibish serve as a stark reminder of what really drove the events of 10/7—the thing that remains at the core of the resistance movement and why Hamas or its likes can't ever be stopped—which is apartheid.

This chapter is supposed to be a timeline of the events that took place during the Gaza Genocide (not that it has stopped at the time of this book's publication). From October 2023 to September 2024 (when I put down my pen and concluded this book), a year has passed since Israel began its invasion of Gaza. Gaza is destroyed, its people are dead, its land is barren, its kids are orphans, its women are widows, its men are martyrs, and its soul is crushed. But Gaza's will remains strong! Many individuals online express sentiments like, "This is what you get when you start a war you can't win," as a response to pictures of dead Gazan children. It's hypocritical how a fake story of forty beheaded babies made the West foam at the mouth while real-life Gazan babies exploding into a dozen pieces doesn't arouse an ounce of Zionist sympathy for the Palestinian plight. So, I'd like to remind my readers that history didn't begin on October 7. It was the result of centuries-long oppression of Palestinians.

In 1878, the first agricultural colony of Zionists was established in Gaza during the reign of Abdulhamid II of the Ottoman Empire. Four years later, 25,000 Jewish-European immigrants settled in Palestine. For Palestinians, it was akin to Native Americans watching Jamestown being established. At the turn of the nineteenth century, the Zionist Congress called for the creation of "a home for the Jewish people" in the middle of Palestine. Zionists kept acquiring more land, and by 1915, Jews made up 6 percent of the population. You'll see far-right fascists in Europe accusing Muslim immigrants of plotting to occupy their country. In fact, these innocent Muslim immigrants are simply victims of colonization. Jews are the ones who used the Great Replacement Theory to plot the conquest of Arab lands. In the words of the Zangwill: "[We] must be prepared either to drive out by the sword the [Arab] tribes in possession, as our forefathers did or to grapple with the problem of a large alien population, mostly Mohammedan, and accustomed for centuries to hate us." (Awan, 2023).

The Balfour Declaration of 1917 made it known to Arabs that Zionists had already made a deal with the Evil One. The very next year, the British took Palestine from the Ottomans. In 1920, Hagana was founded to hunt down Arabs and exterminate them. As Palestinians began protesting against the large-scale immigration of Jews, 67,000 Zionists had entered Palestine by 1928, taking the Hebrew population to 16 percent. It took them a little over a decade to start smuggling arms in at the Jaffa port.

In 1939, we already had the likes of Jabotinsky arguing that "Arabs must make room for the Jews in Eretz Israel." From 1946 to 1948, Zionist terrorists made enemies with the Arabs and the British. They were busy bombing hotels and massacring Arab civilians. The Plan Dalet involved the Deir Yassin massacre, where Jews killed 15,000 men, women, and children without discrimination. The al-Nakbah happened, and legal residents of Palestine had to run for their lives. As the State of Israel declared its ill-gotten and unjustified "independence," Palestinians became the new Native Americans or Aboriginals.

From 1948 to modern times, Israel has been persecuting Palestinians. It has created a situation in Gaza that can only be described as apartheid. That's why Palestinians resist and why Hamas exists. Now, I'll provide a comprehensive timeline of the events that have taken place during the genocide of Gaza and its people. Let it be known that the Israelis have turned into Nazis, and we're seeing a holocaust right in front of our eyes. As Israel marches into the heart of Lebanon to fight Hezbollah and massacre Lebanese people, the West is openly supporting Zionists, both morally and financially.

A Comprehensive Timeline of the Gaza Genocide

October 2023

- **October 7:** Hamas militants attack the Supernova Music Festival.

- **October 8:** Israel declares war for the first time since 1973.

- **October 9:** The Zionist government collectively punishes Gazans by blocking the Gaza Strip ("We are fighting human animals, and we are acting accordingly.").

- **October 10:** Israel begins the massacre of UNRWA workers and civilians in Gaza.

- **October 11:** The Islamic University of Gaza is attacked, and

Jewish settlers start killing random Palestinians.

- **October 12:** America joins the genocide as Israel prevents Gazans from accessing fuel, water, or electricity.

- **October 13:** Gazans are forced to relocate to the south of the enclave.

- **October 15:** The Committee to Protect Journalists reported the death of journalists in Gaza.

- **October 16:** Khan Younis is swamped by 400,000 refugees displaced by Israel's invasion.

- **October 18:** Biden arrives in Tel Aviv while many humanitarian organizations predict the health system will collapse in Gaza.

- **October 19:** Israel destroys the St. Porphyrius Church.

- **October 21:** Hamas releases two hostages to the Red Cross at Qatar's behest.

- **October 22:** Israel hits the al-Ansar Mosque.

- **October 24:** Freed hostage Lifshitz claims she was treated well in captivity.

- **October 25:** Israel targets the family of the journalist Wael al-Dahdouh.

- **October 27:** The United Nations General Assembly passed a resolution that called Israel to work toward an immediate ceasefire and termination of hostilities in Gaza.

- **October 28:** Israel invades Gaza.

- **October 30:** Israel hits the Turkish Palestinian Friendship Hospital.

- **October 31:** Houthis use their new Arrow aerial defense system to launch ballistic missiles toward Israel.

November 2023

- **November 1:** Jabalia refugee camp.

- **November 2:** The siege of Gaza City officially begins.

- **November 3:** Israel hits multiple schools and hospitals.

- **November 4:** Israel hits the Maghazi refugee camp.

- **November 8:** Israel destroys the Khaled bin al-Waleed Mosque.

- **November 10:** Israeli tanks surround the few remaining hospitals in Gaza.

- **November 14:** Israel raids the al-Shifa Hospital.

- **November 15:** Israel attacks the Sabra Mosque.

- **November 17:** Israel attacks the al-Falah School.

- **November 18:** Israel attacks the al-Fakhoora School.

- **November 19:** Doctors at al-Shifa evacuate premature babies from the hospital.

- **November 22:** Israel and Hamas strike a deal to pause fighting for four days.

- **November 24:** The first ceasefire comes into effect.

- **November 25:** Hamas releases thirteen hostages and four Thai nationals.

- **November 26:** Netanyahu visits the Gaza Strip.

December 2023

- **December 1:** IDF resumes its operations in Gaza.

- **December 4:** Israel destroys the Palace of Justice.

- **December 5:** The invasion of Khan Younis begins.

- **December 7:** The poet Refaat Alareer is killed.

- **December 10:** Gaza's Ministry of Health reports 50,000 wounded since October 7.

- **December 12:** The Kamal Adwan Hospital is attacked.

- **December 15:** Israel starts invading Rafah.

- **December 17:** Israel randomly arrests 1,000 Palestinians.

- **December 20:** Ismail Haniyeh goes to Cairo to negotiate a truce with Israel.

- **December 25:** Netanyahu is heckled by the families of the hostages.

- **December 29:** The US sells weapons worth $147.5 million to Israel as South Africa brings Israel to the ICJ on charges of genocide.

January 2024

- **January 2:** Israel attacks the al-Amal Hospital.

- **January 3:** The death toll in Gaza reaches 22,313 (as per Gaza's Health Ministry).

- **January 9:** The Saudi ambassador to the UK shows interest in normalizing relationships with Israel.

- **January 12:** Israel strikes a deal with Qatar to supply medicines to Gaza (but didn't actually give these medicines to Gazans).

- **January 14:** This date marks one hundred years of genocide.

- **January 15:** Houthis decide to attack American and British naval/commercial vessels as well.

- **January 20:** An Israeli is forced to kill an American citizen east of Ramallah.

- **January 21:** Israelis hold protests and demonstrations against Netanyahu's regime.

- **January 22:** Israel attacks the Nasser Hospital.

- **January 14:** Israeli protestors prevent aid trucks from reaching Gaza.

- **January 29:** Hind Rajab is killed.

- **January 31:** The al-Amal Hospital is out of service.

February 2024

- **February 13:** France imposes travel bans on Israeli settlers who attacked Palestinian civilians in the West Bank.

- **February 14:** Israel launches its heaviest attack on Lebanon.

- **February 15:** Egypt starts a refugee camp south of Rafah.

- **February 23:** UNRWA is left unable to provide its services in Gaza.

- **February 25:** Aaron Bushnell sets himself on fire.

- **February 26:** Israel attacks Baalbek, Lebanon.

- **February 29:** Israel opens fire on a crowd and kills civilians as New Zealand designates Hamas as a terrorist entity.

March 2024

- **March 2:** Houthis sink the MV *Rubymar*.

- **March 7:** An Israeli authority plans to build 3,500 new illegal settlements in the West Bank.

- **March 9:** Pro-Netanyahu protestors in Tel Aviv call for the "total burning of Gaza."

- **March 10:** Israeli settlers destroy the Bab al-Rahma Cemetery.

- **March 13:** Israelis attack the Jenin Government Hospital.

- **March 18:** Israel raids the al-Shifa Hospital.

- **March 25:** The British Royal Air Force provides ten metric tons of food supplies to Gazans.

April 2024

- **April 10:** Israel kills the descendants of Ismail Haniyeh as Ireland declares recognition of a future Palestinian state.

- **April 12:** Many Western countries prevent their cities from traveling to Israel.

- **April 13:** Iran launches dozens of drones toward Israel.

- **April 14:** Jewish settlers uproot thirty olive trees.

- **April 19:** Barbados officially recognizes the Palestinian state.

- **April 21:** A mass grave is discovered at the Nasser Medical Complex.

- **April 23:** Jamaica officially recognizes the Palestinian state.

May 2024

- **May 2:** Colombia breaks ties with Israel.

- **May 5:** Israel moves against al-Jazeera.

- **May 7:** The Rafah Offensive begins as Israel invades this territory.

- **May 9:** A total of seven mass graves are discovered at the al-Shifa.

- **May 10:** Jewish extremists burn down UNRWA's headquarters.

- **May 20:** The ICC issues arrest warrants for the Hamas and Israeli top leadership.

- **May 21:** Israeli forces prevent the Associated Press (AP) from covering its military operations.

- **May 22:** Spain, Ireland, and Norway announce their willingness to recognize Palestine as a state.

- **May 26:** Tel al-Sultan airstrikes cause massive civilian casualties and burnings.

- **May 28:** The shelling of the al-Mawasi Tent Camp takes place.

- **May 31:** As Israel withdraws from Jabalia, 70 percent of the refugee camp is left destroyed.

June 2024

- **June 6:** Israel attacks yet another school in Nuseirat.

- **June 8:** Israel rescues four hostages after killing over 270 Palestinians and wounding almost 700.

- **June 17:** Netanyahu dissolved Israel's war cabinet.

- **June 21:** Armenia recognizes Palestine as a state.

- **June 25:** Hamas uses a Chinese Pakistani missile to attack Israel.

- **June 27:** Israel attacks the al-Shuja'iyya neighborhood.

- **June 29:** The Arab League removes Hamas from the list of recognized terrorist organizations.

July 2024

- **July 1:** Israel releases the people captured from the al-Shia Hospital due to the lack of evidence against them.

- **July 3:** Israeli forces torture and kill a Palestinian man with Down Syndrome.

- **July 9:** The al-Awda school massacre takes place.

- **July 13:** Israel attacks the al-Mawasi area and kills civilians.

- **July 23:** Japan sanctions Israeli settlers for the first time in history.

- **July 26:** The Khadija school airstrike takes place.

- **July 29:** Nine Israeli soldiers are arrested for sexually abusing Palestinian detainees.

- **July 31:** Israel assassinates Ismail Haniyeh.

August 2024

- **August 3:** Israel bombs the Hamama School.

- **August 9:** Israel invades Khan Younis again.

- **August 10:** Israel bombs the al-Tabaeen School.

- **August 14:** Israel prepares to establish more illegal settlements in Bethlehem.

September 2024

- **September 4:** Greta Thunberg is arrested during a pro-Palestinian protest.

- **September 11:** Israel attacks the al-Jawni school building.

- **September 17:** Israel remotely explodes the pagers used by Hezbollah fighters in Lebanon.

- **September 21:** Israel attacks the Zeitoun School in Gaza City.

- **September 27:** Hezbollah commander Hassan Nasrallah is assassinated.

- **September 30:** Israel attacks Yemeni ports in control of the Houthis while killing PFLP militants in Lebanon (who had no part in the entire Israel-Hamas conflict).

Conclusion

"The only moral thing Palestinian civilians can do, apparently, is to die. The only legal thing the rest of us can do is to watch them die. And be silent. If not, we risk our scholarships, grants, lecture fees, and livelihoods." — Arundhati Roy.

In the final days of the Apartheid-era South Africa (before it eventually collapsed in 1990), the White-run government of the African nation overthrew the government in neighboring Angola, installed a puppet regime in nearby Namibia, invaded Zimbabwe, attacked Botswana, and even created hostilities with a third neighbor, Zambia. Suffice it to say, it didn't work, and the apartheid regime had to breathe its last soon after, at the hands of the movement started by Nelson Mandela—a man considered a dangerous terrorist by the US up until the late 2000s.

As Israel has attacked Houthi-controlled Yemeni seaports and launched a full-scale invasion of Southern Lebanon (a repetition of a similar military adventure that caused the rise of Hamas in the eighties), we can see the apartheid regime breathing its last. Without US support and EU-supplied arms, Israel's far-right government can't sustain even a single war. A report states that more than 46,000 businesses have gone bankrupt due to Israel's war with Hamas (Korn, 2024), and more businesses are expected to close in the wake of Netanyahu's misadventures in Lebanon.

A country that couldn't sustain fighting a single militant organization (i.e., Hamas) can't survive a battle with two (i.e., Hamas and Hezbollah)! Time is up for Israel. The victory of the Palestinians draws closer. It shouldn't surprise anyone that Palestinians can win. After all, world history is filled with stories of many brave and courageous nations gaining victory over their oppressors. From Haiti to Indonesia—victims of colonialism have always risen as victors in the end. Cubans, Vietnamese, South Africans, Algerians, their neighbors, the Libyans, Egyptians, Malaysians, and various other nations successfully thwarted their White masters and became independent in the end. That's how we look at the issue of Palestine as well. It's not a battle between Islam and Judaism—as Zionists would like to portray it—but a war between tyrants from Europe and their indigenous victims. It's the David and Goliath story once again. It repeated itself when Native Americans and African Americans were fighting for their rights against White invaders, and it's repeating itself with Gazans fighting for their right of self-determination against Zionist Jews.

A Churchill quote regarding this issue is making the rounds on the internet. Extracted from a 1937 Palestinian Commission (and repeated in the UK Parliament, further testifying to its authenticity), this quote goes like this: "*I do not admit that a dog in the manger has the final right to the manger, even though he may have lain there for a very long time. I do not admit, for instance, that a great wrong has been done to the Red Indians of America or the Black people of Australia. I do not admit that a wrong has been done to those people by the fact that a stronger race, a higher grade race, or, at any rate, a more worldly-wise race, to put it that way, has come in and taken their place.*" In simple words, Mr. Winston Churchill was of an opinion shared by White and Jewish supremacists alike, i.e., a "superior race" has the right to take your land, subjugate you, dictate your law, and receive your 100 percent surrender. A superior race has the right to replace an inferior race. That was the policy of White colonizers and Zionists. Even today, the West acts like it has abandoned its past (pretending that Hitler was an anomaly without trying to give a reasonable argument as to what made millions of Germans support Hitler in the first place). However, it becomes apparent from their support for (and almost sensual obsession with) Israel that the colonizers of the past haven't changed one bit. I, for once, can't believe in this Western propaganda that Germans turned fascists all of a sudden, supported Nazis, massacred Jews, were defeated by Russians (a fact your teachers won't share with you so often in school), and then became good people.

However, the spiritual successors of Hitler, Leopold II (this bastard was the self-styled sole owner of the Congolese people), and Churchill live on, and Palestinians have allies in the US and the EU as well. Now, we have many Americans and Europeans supporting the cause of the Palestinians as they realize that Israel is but an apartheid regime run by fascists. We have the likes of Greta Thunberg (McGowan, 2023), who realize that the problem of climate change is strongly related to the problem of colonialism, the darkest example of which is Israel's apartheid against Palestinians. So, her gradual policy shift has turned young Greta from a climate change activist beloved by the elites of Europe into a "rebel" who openly talks about the wrongs of colonialism. That's what happens when you realize the truth. Just as in the Matrix movies, the moment you realize the truth about the world, the machines turn on you. In real life, the moment you see how Zionists are controlling everything and destroying this world out of sheer self-interest, the media and entire world governments become your enemy.

That's what happened to Fidel Castro, the man who survived 638 attempts on his life (Oppmann, 2016)—and the Zionist media boasts about it as if they weren't breaking several key international laws by trying to kill a political leader. Castro realized that Zionism was the true ruling party in the US. In his eloquent and thought-provoking words, he described Democrats and Republicans as soft and hard powers of Zionists in America, respectively. I will say that Democrats sell you Zionism with flowers, Republicans will sell it to you with guns, and Israelis will present it to you via blonde Russian/Ukrainian models.

We also have the example of the brave journalist Sarah Wilkinson, who has cops breaking into her home, smashing her stuff, and detaining her just for the "crime" of being anti-Zionist. Well, when you genuinely realize who your *true masters* are, you get imprisoned! Unmasking those who are running this world isn't allowed. By that, I am not repeating the same old anti-Semitic tropes of Jews running the world. No, Jews don't run the world. Jews are not the enemy! Zionists are the enemy. A Zionist can be anyone. They can be Jewish, Muslim, Hindu, Christian, or even atheist (interestingly, the early ones didn't believe in God). We have Hindu Zionists in India who want nothing with their lives but to immigrate to Israel and murder Muslims. Most Zionists in America happen to be Christians. We also have Muslim Zionists who love the country of Israel as if it weren't the perfect embodiment of all the criticism they level against Islam. I saw one of such shameless Muslim Zionists, by the name of Imtiaz, sharing an Islamophobic picture on the X site (formerly Twitter), mocking Palestinian refugees. It was a cartoonish depiction of two Palestinian refugees seeking shelter and knocking on the door of Egypt while yelling, "*Open the door!*" A man from Egypt responds, "*We're not home.*" It reminded me of the Nazi propaganda against Jews during the thirties. These Muslim Zionists are the versions of "self-hating Jews" in the Muslim circle.

However, Zionism is failing quickly. "Project Israel" is doomed. In the words of Khomeini, the days of Israel are numbered. Khamenei predicted that 2040 would be the last year of Israel's existence. We can see that the end of apartheid will be much sooner than 2040! You might ridicule this statement, calling it a very usual "political claim" made by statesmen against enemies. Well, earlier in September, a top general in Israel named Yitzhak Brik said that it was Israel that was collapsing, not Hamas (Brik, 2024). His analysis is that Israeli forces grow weaker day by day while Hamas replenishes its ranks with young recruits aged seventeen and eighteen. Also, Israeli reservists are becoming restless and unwilling to be drafted (360,000 of them had to join the army in October). Conscripted soldiers are exhausted since a lack of training degrades their professional skills and their warrior spirit (Rubin & Soroka, 2024). As a result, a retired IDF general (reserves) warns that: "*Israel's economy, international relations, and social cohesiveness are severely damaged by this war of attrition against both Hamas and Hezbollah.*"

The genocide of the Gazans is turning people against Zionists. Israelis are losing face in the war. Just imagine the horror of killing a young man with Down Syndrome after launching attack dogs at him. I'm sharing an image of M. Bhar, the twenty-four-year-old man who "died a lonely death," as reported by the BBC. The headline was written to obscure the role of the Israeli military in Bhar's death. The 3D image shows the innocent Bhar being mauled by an Israeli canine while he gently instructs the dog to let go of him. Bhar is just one of the many victims of Israeli aggression. From the timeline, you can see that even Israeli settlers are involved in massacring Palestinians. Thousands of Palestinians have died at the hands of the IDF just for the crime of existing. But the days of dehumanization and persecution are over, if not in my lifetime, then in the age of my descendants! One day, we'll liberate Palestine and live in peace on the land of our forefathers.

Final Remarks on the Palestinian Struggle for Independence

> "*At the level of individuals, violence is a cleansing force. It frees the native from his inferiority complex and from his despair and inaction; it makes him fearless and restores his self-respect.*" — Frantz Fanon.

Many Latin American nations have expressed solidarity with the Palestinians because we all believe in the same ideals—the need to escape the clutches of colonialism through armed resistance. The teaching of F. Fanon says that the very idea that violence is only acceptable by the state and unacceptable for anyone who opposes it is a racist and colonialist idea. Freedom is gained not by appealing to the morality of the enemy but by fighting back. Coming back to the two quotes we shared at the front of this book, freedom is never gained by a nation peacefully.

Anyone who is depriving us of peace doesn't deserve peaceful dialogue. Liberals who oppose the armed struggle of Palestinians historically opposed the armed resistance of many other nations. They have criticized Vietnamese, Cubans, and South Africans. They opposed resistance fighters like Malcolm X and the Black Panthers, who are now considered heroes. Similarly, those criticizing the Palestinian self-determination movement will become our supporters after we win.

The resilience of the people of Gaza is a profound testament to their durable spirit in the face of relentless adversity. The history of this tiny strip is marked by hardships. Apartheid, persecution, dehumanization, human rights abuses, and countless genocides prevented Gazans from showcasing their full potential. However, they never backed down from expressing their willingness to make waves in the history of the world. As a Zionism-infested world dehumanizes them and openly mocks them, they hold their heads high.

The destruction of schools by military actions aims to undermine the Palestinian spirit, yet many students persist in their pursuit of knowledge. For instance, despite the loss of lives and the destruction of educational facilities, students have achieved remarkable academic success under dire circumstances. Some experts have opined that resilience among Gazans is closely linked to positive emotional states such as enthusiasm and determination. Studies show that individuals with higher levels of social support and spiritual well-being exhibit greater resilience, even amidst the distress caused by the ongoing siege.

As Zionists mock their struggle and make fun of their dead children, Gazans use this mockery to fuel their passion and their ambition to set their country free. The world may have forgotten, but this isn't the first time that Gaza has faced starvation. It's not the first time that Israel has invaded the homeland of Gazans in the guise of "erasing terrorism," only to detain their men, rape their women, kill their children, slay their animals, demolish their homes, harass their neighbors, and maim anyone who dares criticize the tyranny.

Living under apartheid is a nightmare, but we await the sunrise. In the words of the famous poet Faiz:

We shall see ...

When these high mountains of tyranny and oppression
turn to fluff and evaporate.

And we oppressed, beneath our feet, will have this earth
shiver, shake, and beat ...

We shall see.

Appendix I

Statistical Data on Gaza's Population, Economy, and Humanitarian Indicators

This appendix provides comprehensive statistical data to offer readers a better understanding of the socio-economic context of Gaza, highlighting key indicators related to population, economic conditions, and humanitarian challenges.

Population Statistics

- **Total Population**: Approximately 2.2 million people lived in the Gaza Strip as of August 2024.

- **Population Density**: Gaza has one of the highest population densities in the world, with about 6,102 individuals per square kilometer.

- **Demographics**: A significant portion of the population comprises refugees, contributing to demographic pressures on resources and services.

Economic Indicators

- **Poverty Rate**: As of mid-2023, the overall poverty rate in Gaza was estimated at nearly 64 percent, compared to approximately 12 percent in the West Bank. This reflects a significant increase from previous years.

- **Unemployment Rate**: The unemployment rate in Gaza reached about 57 percent in early 2024, a dramatic rise from 45.3 percent reported in 2022.

- **GDP per Capita**: In 2023, Gaza's GDP per capita was recorded at approximately $929, marking a historical low and a 28 percent drop from the previous year.

- **Economic Contraction**: The Palestinian economy experienced an estimated contraction of 8.7 percent in real GDP for 2023, with projections indicating a potential decline of up to 25.8 percent in 2024 due to ongoing conflict and economic disruptions.

Humanitarian Indicators

- **Food Insecurity**: By early 2024, approximately 55 percent of households in northern Gaza were experiencing catastrophic food insecurity, with expectations for this figure to rise further if conflicts continue.

- **Health Infrastructure Damage**: The ongoing conflict has severely damaged health facilities, exacerbating the public health crises and reducing access to essential medical care.

- **Human Development Index (HDI)**: The ongoing conflict is projected to result in setbacks of over twenty years in human development progress for the region.

Employment and Economic Activity

- **Job Losses**: Since October 2023, around 200,000 jobs have been lost in Gaza alone due to economic disruptions caused by the conflict.

- **Minimum Wage**: As of 2022, the minimum monthly wage was set at approximately 697 NIS, which has been insufficient to meet rising living costs amid economic challenges.

Appendix II

Bibliography of Further Reading and Resources

This bibliography provides a curated list of books, articles, reports, and online resources for readers interested in exploring the socio-economic, historical, and humanitarian contexts of Gaza and the broader Palestinian issue.

Books

- *Gaza: An Inquest into Its Martyrdom,* by Norman Finkelstein, is a critical examination of the political and humanitarian situation in Gaza.

- *The Gaza Strip: The Political Economy of De-Development,* by Sara Roy, provides an in-depth analysis of the economic conditions in Gaza and the impact of Israeli policies.

- *Hamas: A History from Within,* by Azzam Tamimi, gives us very careful insight into the political dynamics and history of Hamas within the context of Gaza.

- *The Iron Wall: Israel and the Arab World,* by Avi Shlaim, is a very comprehensive overview of Israeli Arab relations, including the situation in Gaza.

- *Palestine: Peace Not Apartheid,* by ex-President Carter, discusses the Israeli-Palestinian conflict with a focus on peace efforts.

Articles and Reports

- *The Humanitarian Impact of the Blockade on Gaza* (United Nations Office for the Coordination of Humanitarian Affairs (OCHA)) is a detailed report on the humanitarian situation in Gaza due to the blockade.

- *Gaza's Economy: The Impact of Conflict and Blockade* (World Bank) is a deep analysis of the economic conditions in Gaza, with statistical data.

- *The Situation in Gaza: Facts and Figures* (UNRWA (United Nations Relief and Works Agency) offers insights into living conditions and humanitarian needs in Gaza.

- *The Right to Food in Gaza: A Human Rights Perspective* (Human Rights Watch) discusses food security issues within a human rights framework.

Online Resources

- **B'Tselem** (https://www.btselem.org/): The Israeli Information Center for Human Rights in the Occupied Territories provides reports and data on human rights issues in Gaza and other occupied territories.

- **Al Jazeera English** (https://www.aljazeera.com/): Gaza Conflict Coverage offers news articles, documentaries, and analyses of ongoing events in Gaza.

- **Palestinian Central Bureau of Statistics** (http://www.pcbs.gov.ps/): It's an ideal source for data on demographics, economy, and social indicators in Palestine.

Documentaries

- *Gaza: A History of Violence* (2019) — A documentary exploring the historical context of violence in Gaza.

- *The War Around Us* (2014) — Chronicles life during the 2008-2009 Gaza War through the eyes of journalists.

Appendix III

The Cost of Human Life in the Gazan Genocide

According to the Palestinian Ministry of Health and various reports, here is a summary of the casualties and other statistics related to the ongoing conflict in Gaza:

Casualties

- **Total Palestinian Deaths in Gaza**: Over 43,000 (as per an estimation by the Jewish press) and at least 119,000 (as per the latest report by US health workers).

- **Civilian Deaths**: Approximately 32,000, including 17,000 children and 11,000 women (again, all these stats come from the Western media).

- **Deaths in the West Bank**: Over 650 Palestinians.

- **Deaths in Israel**: Approximately 1,200, including about 860 civilians (in the Supernova Festival, where most of these deaths occurred at the hands of Israeli jets).

- **Deaths in Lebanon**: Thousands have died, and the death toll continues due to Israeli terrorism.

- **Healthcare Workers Killed**: Over 500.

- **Journalists Killed**: At least 116.

Injuries

- **Injured Palestinians in Gaza**: Approximately 92,401.

- **Injured Palestinians in the West Bank**: Over 5,400.

- **Injured Israeli Terrorists**: About 2,206.

Displacement and Humanitarian Conditions

- **Displaced Palestinians in Gaza**: Nearly 1.9 million (about 86 percent of the pre-war population).

- **Food Insecurity**: Approximately 1.1 million people (half of the population is facing catastrophic food insecurity).

Infrastructure Damage

- **Percentage of Buildings Damaged or Destroyed**: Estimated at about 59.3 percent, with over 60 percent of homes affected.

- **Schools Damaged**: Around 85 percent of school buildings have been affected.

Additional Statistics

- **Missing Persons**: An estimated 7,000 people are missing, presumed dead under rubble.

- **Economic Impact**: The conflict has led to unprecedented unemployment rates, with estimates suggesting that over half a million jobs have been lost across the occupied Palestinian territory due to the war.

Acknowledgments

The author would like to express profound gratitude to all who contributed to the creation of this book, including researchers, activists, publisher /and individuals whose stories have enriched our understanding of Gaza's history and struggle. Thanks to Nicole Kaye Talento for pencil drawingsincluded in the book. Special thanks go to those who sacrificed their lives to see the Palestinian flag unfurled worldwide, from the hands of students at Columbia University to the streets of Colombia and the University of Sydney.

References

1. Abraham, G., "At the Cliff of Death: A Poem from Gaza," *Mizna Online*, March 25, 2024, https://mizna.org/literary/haya-abu-nasser/.

2. Abunimah, A., "Israeli lawmaker's call for genocide of Palestinians gets thousands Of Facebook Likes," *The Electronic Intifada*, February 12, 2017, https://electronicintifada.net/blogs/ali-abunimah/israeli-lawmakers-call-genocide-palestinians-gets-thousands-facebook-likes.

3. Afp, "Israel bombs Gaza during Muslim festival despite US rebuke," *Business Recorder*, April 10, 2024, https://www.brecorder.com/news/40298096.

4. Ageel, G., "While the world has abandoned Gaza, its doctors have done the opposite. They are our heroes," *The Guardian*, November 25, 2023, https://www.theguardian.com/commentisfree/2023/nov/25/world-abandoned-gaza-doctors-heroes-palestinian-hospitals.

5. Agencies, "Activist Tamimi freed from Israeli detention," *DAWN. COM*, December 1, 2023, https://www.dawn.com/news/1794077.

6. AJLabs, "Israel-Gaza war in maps and charts: Live tracker," *Al Jazeera*, August 19, 2024, https://www.aljazeera.com/news/longform/2023/10/9/israel-hamas-war-in-maps-and-charts-live-tracker.

7. Al-Kassab, F, "A top U.N. court says Gaza genocide is 'plausible' but does not order cease-fire," *NPR*, January 26, 2024, https://www.npr.org/2024/01/26/1227078791/icj-israel-genocide-gaza-palestinians-south-africa.

8. Alam, M. S., "A land without a people," Palgrave Macmillan US eBooks, 2009,https://doi.org/10.1057/9780230101371_8.

9. Almeghari, R., "Making Music in Gaza: Young musician strikes a chord with Gaza's instrument store," *The New Arab*, August 29, 2018, https://www.newarab.com/analysis/young-musician-strikes-chord-gazas-instrument-store.

10. Amer, R., "Gaza's terrified children all too aware Israel's bombs steal their joy," *Al Jazeera*, October 17, 2023, https://www.aljazeera.com/news/2023/10/13/gazas-terrified-children-all-too-aware-israels-bombs-stole-their-joy.

11. Amnesty International, "Israel's apartheid against Palestinians," *Amnesty.org*, August 12, 2024, https://www.amnesty.org/en/latest/campaigns/2022/02/israels-system-of-apartheid/.

12. Anabel, S. N., "Why are people on TikTok comparing this Palestinian girl to Anne Frank?" *Anabel Magazine*, October 29, 2023, https://www.anabelmagazine.com/news/72683/pse-njerezit-ne-tiktok-po-e-krahasojne-kete-vajze-palestineze-me-anne-frank/eng.

13. Armstrong, B. K., "Wael Al-Dahdouh: Al Jazeera reporter's family killed in Gaza strike," *BBC.com, October 26, 2023*, https://www.bbc.com/news/world-middle-east-67225204.

14. Awan, A. N., "The hidden history of Hamas," *The National Interest*, November 14, 2023, https://nationalinterest.org/feature/hidden-history-hamas-207266.

15. Azulay, M., "Netanyahu says no Palestinian state if he remains PM," *Ynetnews.com, March 16, 2015*, http://www.ynetnews.com/articles/0,7340,L-4637673,00.html.

16. Baker, A. M., "The psychological impact of the Intifada on Palestinian children in the occupied West Bank and Gaza: An exploratory study," *American Journal of Orthopsychiatry*, 60(4), 496—505, 1990, https://doi.org/10.1037/h0079207.

17. Balevic, K., "Gaza's unemployment is nearing 80 percent as one

disaster compounds another, UN says," *Business Insider*, June 8, 2024, https://www.businessinsider.com/gazas-unemployment-soars-children-work-feed-families-un-2024-6.

18. Bartov, O., "As a former IDF soldier and historian of genocide, I was deeply disturbed by my recent visit to Israel," *The Guardian*, August 15, 2024, https://www.theguardian.com/world/article/2024/aug/13/israel-gaza-historian-omer-bartov.

19. Bauck, W., "'It connects people:' Palestinian chefs are using food to share their stories," *The Guardian*, December 12, 2023, https://www.theguardian.com/environment/2023/dec/12/palestine-chef-food-recipe-gaza-israel-war.

20. Ben-Ami, Shlomo, *Prophets without Honor: The Untold Story of the 2000 Camp David Summit and the Making of Today's Middle East* (New York, 2022), https://doi.org/10.1093/oso/9780190060473.003.0019

21. Ben-Israel, H., "Debates with Toynbee: Herzog, Talmon, Friedman," *Israel Studies*, 2006, 11(1), 79—90. http://www.jstor.org/stable/30245780

22. Berg, R., "ICJ says Israeli occupation of Palestinian territories is illegal," *BBC.com*, July 19, 2024, https://www.bbc.com/news/articles/cjerjzxlpvdo.

23. Boffey, D., "'From the river to the sea:' Where does the slogan come from and what does it mean?" *The Guardian*, November 16, 2023, https://www.theguardian.com/world/2023/oct/31/from-the-river-to-the-sea-where-does-the-slogan-come-from-and-what-does-it-mean-israel-palestine.

24. Bouranova, A., "Is Israel Committing Genocide in Gaza? New Report from BU School of Law's International Human Rights Clinic Lays Out Case," *Boston University*, July 25, 2024, https://www.bu.edu/articles/2024/is-israel-committing-genocide-in-gaza/.

25. Brabenec, R., "The most tragic victims in the Israel-Hamas war are those who have no say in it," *Tennessee Lookout,* February 21, 2024, https://tennesseelookout.com/2024/02/20/the-most-tragic-victims-in-the-israel-hamas-war-are-those-who-have-no-say-in-it/.

26. Brik, Yitzhak, "Opinion | It Is Not Hamas That Is Collapsing, but Israel," *Haaretz,* September 3, 2024. https://www.haaretz.com/opinion/2024-09-03/ty-article-opinion/.premium/it-is-not-hamas-that-is-collapsing-but-israel/00000191-b3bf-dffe-abf9-bfffd0a50000.

27. Byman, D., & Duff, D., "What has Hamas achieved since Oct. 7?" *Foreign Policy,* December 18, 2023, https://foreignpolicy.com/2023/12/18/hamas-success-israel-gaza-war-achievements-cost/.

28. Camut, N., "Israel minister suspended after calling nuking Gaza an option," *POLITICO,* November 5, 2023, https://www.politico.eu/article/israel-minister-amichai-eliyahu-suspend-benjamin-netanyahu-nuclear-bomb-gaza-hamas-war/.

29. Canada Talks Israel/Palestine, Edward Said on whether Jews have a claim to Palestine," December 15, 2015YouTube, 0:2:14, https://www.youtube.com/watch?v=-MbXY3X-xGU.

30. Catherine Vargas Films, "Watch this awesome Palestinian Wedding Dabke Dance Atlanta," July 25, 2022, YouTube, 0:1:56, https://www.youtube.com/watch?v=iy_pZH7e0FY.

31. Curtis, M. C., "Is Israel committing genocide in Gaza?" *Slate Magazine,* January 18, 2024, https://slate.com/news-and-politics/2024/01/israel-genocide-gaza-palestine-hamas-war-trial.html.

32. Davis, C. R., "Israel wants Palestinians to rise up against Hamas. One who did says that's now impossible," *Business Insider,* October 15, 2023, https://www.businessinsider.com/rami-aran-palestinians-cannot-fight-hamas-while-under-israeli-attack-2023-10

33. Erakat, N., "No, Israel does not have the right to Self-Defense in international law against occupied Palestinian territory," *Jadaliyya - ةيلادج,،،* July 10, 2017, https://www.jadaliyya.com/Details/27551.

34. Oxfam International, "Failing Gaza: undrinkable water, no access to toilets and little hope on the horizon," *Oxfam International* May 25, 2022, https://www.oxfam.org/en/failing-gaza-undrinkable-water-no-access-toilets-and-little-hope-horizon

35. Fatima, Y., "The language of genocide: How Israel dehumanizes Palestinians," *DAWN.COM*, November 7, 2023, https://www.dawn.com/news/1786922.

36. Fayyad, H., "Gaza's Great March of Return protests explained," *Al Jazeera*, March 30, 2019, https://www.aljazeera.com/news/2019/3/30/gazas-great-march-of-return-protests-explained.

37. Filiu, J., "The self-immolation of Aaron Bushnell, an 'extreme protest' for Palestine in Washington," *Le Monde.fr, March 4, 2024*, https://www.lemonde.fr/en/international/article/2024/03/04/the-self-immolation-of-aaron-bushnell-an-extreme-protest-for-palestine-in-washington_6581762_4.html.

38. Fisk, R., "I spoke to Palestinians who still hold the keys to homes they fled decades ago—many are still determined to return," *The Independent. The Independent*, June 28, 2018, https://www.independent.co.uk/voices/palestine-keys-return-home-israel-palestinians-a8398341.html.

39. Flatley, D., "Hamas Faces Few Sanctions for a Group Called Terrorist by the US," *Bloomberg*, October 24, 2024, https://www.bloomberg.com/news/articles/2023-10-24/slim-roster-of-hamas-sanctions-reflects-challenge-five-charts.

40. Reliefweb, "For Palestinians in the West Bank, 2023 was the deadliest year on record," *ReliefWeb*, December 15, 2023, https://reliefweb.int/report/occupied-palestinian-territory/palestinians-west-bank-2023-was-deadliest-year-record.

41. Forward, "So what does 'intifada' actually mean?" *The Forward*, December 16, 2023, https://forward.com/culture/573654/intifada-arabic-israeli-hamas-war-meaning-linguistics/.

42. Ghanem, N., "Database exposes 500 instances of Israeli incitement to genocide in Gaza," *TRTWORLD*, January 5, 2024, https://www.trtworld.com/middle-east/database-exposes-500-instances-of-israeli-incitement-to-genocide-in-gaza-16537146.

43. Goichman, R., "English-language Wikipedia editors concluded: Israel committing genocide in Gaza," *Haaretz.com*, August 8, 2024, https://www.haaretz.com/israel-news/2024-08-08/ty-article/.premium/english-wikipedia-editors-concluded-israel-is-committing-genocide-in-gaza/00000191-321a-d4dc-a397-bf1e3fba0000.

44. Gold, H., "Israeli minister says there's 'no such thing as a Palestinian people,' inviting US rebuke," *CNN*, March 21, 2023, https://edition.cnn.com/2023/03/21/middleeast/israel-smotrich-palestinians-intl/index.html.

45. Graham-Harrison, E., & Helm, T., "Netanyahu defies Biden, insisting there's 'no space' for Palestinian state," *The Guardian*, January 21, 2024, https://www.theguardian.com/world/2024/jan/20/netanyahu-defies-biden-insisting-theres-no-space-for-palestinian-state.

46. Gridwork, "History didn't begin on Oct. 7," *In These Times*, December 6, 2023, https://inthesetimes.com/article/israel-occupation-palestine-settlers-apartheid-checkpoints-resistance.

47. Haddad, M., "Mapping Israeli occupation," *Al Jazeera*, May 19, 2021, https://www.aljazeera.com/news/2021/5/18/mapping-israeli-occupation-gaza-palestine.

48. Haddad, M., & Chughtai, A., "Israel-Palestine conflict: A brief history in maps and charts," *Al Jazeera*, November 29, 2023, https://www.aljazeera.com/news/2023/11/27/palestine-and-israel-brief-history-maps-and-charts.

49. Hagedorn, E., "US unveils sanctions on Hamas spokesperson Abu Ubaida," *Al-Monitor*, April 12, 2024, https://www.al-monitor.com/originals/2024/04/us-unveils-sanctions-hamas-spokesperson-abu-ubaida.

50. Halileh, S. O., Daoud, A. R., Khatib, R. A., & Mikki-Samarah, N. S., "The impact of the Intifada on the health of a nation," *Taylor and Francis Online, 2002,* https://doi.org/10.1080/13623690208409632.

51. Hindeleh, B., & Saarinen, N., "How big is the Gaza Strip? Here's how the tiny enclave compares to Australia and the world," *ABC News*, October 24, 2023, https://www.abc.net.au/news/2023-10-24/how-big-is-the-gaza-strip/103001830.

52. Hockstader, L., "Palestinians Find Heroes in Hamas," *Washington Post*, August 10, 2001, https://www.washingtonpost.com/archive/politics/2001/08/11/palestinians-find-heroes-in-hamas/36d3d4d9-4282-4a44-96f8-89ba8fa202d8/.

53. Holmes, O., & Balousha, H., "Israeli forces shoot 16 Palestinian protesters at Gaza frontier," *The Guardian*, May 15, 2019, https://www.theguardian.com/world/2019/may/15/israeli-forces-shoot-16-palestinian-protesters-at-gaza-frontier.

54. Humaid, M., "'We want to return to our lands without bloodshed or bombs,'" *Al Jazeera*, March 30, 2018, https://www.aljazeera.com/features/2018/3/30/we-want-to-return-to-our-lands-without-bloodshed-or-bombs.

55. Ibrahim, T., "The Sounds of Palestine," *Medium*, March 30, 2022, https://tasneem-ibrahim.medium.com/the-sounds-of-palestine-3f559fe2fd67.

56. Ishisaka, N., "Understanding Gaza: Don't fall into the trap of dehumanization," *The Seattle Times*, November 6, 2023, https://www.seattletimes.com/seattle-news/understanding-gaza-dont-fall-into-the-trap-of-dehumanization/.

57. Issacharoff, A., "Poll: Barghouti would defeat Abbas and Haniyeh in vote for Palestinian president," *Haaretz.com*, June 27, 2012, https://www.haaretz.com/2012-06-27/ty-article/.premium/poll-barghouti-would-win-pa-elections/0000017f-df1e-d856-a37f-ff-deca6f0000.

58. Itkowitz, C., "Two WWII veterans met in a nursing home. But one had a secret: He fought for Hitler," *Washington Post*, January 6, 2016, https://www.washingtonpost.com/local/two-world-war-ii-vets-who-fought-on-opposite-sides-have-created-a-bond/2016/01/06/2629e11a-aa4b-11e5-bff5-905b92f5f94b_story.html.

59. Jane, M., "John Jay showcases stunning art inspired by brutal repression in South Korea," *W42ST,* October 17, 2022, https://w42st.com/post/john-jay-showcases-art-inspired-by-1980-south-korea-repression/.

60. Jazeera, A., "Students vow to continue Gaza protests after California, Texas arrests," *Al Jazeera*, April 25, 2024, https://www.aljazeera.com/news/2024/4/25/students-arrested-in-california-texas-as-gaza-war-protests-in-us-intensify.

61. Khoury, J., "Hezbollah's Nasrallah praises 'heroic' Oct 7 Hamas attack, says it was '100% Palestinian,'" *Haaretz.com*, November 3, 2023, https://www.haaretz.com/israel-news/2023-11-03/ty-article/hezbollahs-nasrallah-praises-heroic-oct-7-hamas-attack-says-it-was-100-palestinian/0000018b-95a4-db71-a7df-fded25b30000.

62. Kmaneck, R., & Kmaneck, R., "Why has Israel rejected three-phase ceasefire deal accepted by Hamas? What comes next?" *Firstpost*, May 7, 2024, https://www.firstpost.com/explainers/israel-three-phase-ceasefire-deal-hamas-rafah-operation-war-13767918.html.

63. Korn, J., "On Tel Aviv's once-bustling Dizengoff, business owners lament another casualty of war," *Times of Israel*, July 26, 2024, https://www.timesofisrael.com/on-tel-avivs-once-bustling-dizen-

goff-business-owners-lament-another-casualty-of-war/.

64. Kraft, S., "Extremists pay tribute to killer of 48 at funeral," *Los Angeles Times*, March 6, 2019, https://www.latimes.com/archives/la-xpm-1994-02-28-mn-28250-story.html.

65. Krauss, J., "Palestinians fear repeat of 1948 as Israel calls for evacuation," *AP News*, October 14, 2023, https://apnews.com/article/israel-palestinians-gaza-evacuation-history-nakba-a1bec-1ee3477573e80b39b4044a48111.

66. Kuttab, D., "Opinion: Reality check—intifada has nothing to do with the genocide of Jews," *LA Times*, December 12, 2023, https://www.latimes.com/opinion/story/2023-12-12/antisemi-tism-elise-stefanik-genocide-intifada-college-presidents.

67. Lamb, C., "New Mandela or terrorist? Marwan Barghouti's fate could end Gaza war," *The Sunday Times*, August 31, 2024, https://www.thetimes.com/world/israel-hamas-war/article/new-man-dela-or-terrorist-marwan-barghoutis-fate-could-end-gaza-war-mnc38crjb.

68. Laub, K., "Palestinian poll shows a rise in Hamas support, close to 90%," *AP News*, December 13, 2023, https://apnews.com/article/israel-hamas-palestinians-opinion-poll-wartime-views-a0baad-e915619cd070b5393844bc4514.

69. Lavi, T., & Solomon, Z., "Palestinian Youth of the Intifada: PTSD and future orientation," *Journal of the American Academy of Child & Adolescent Psychiatry, 44(11), 1176–1183*, November, 2005, https://doi.org/10.1097/01.chi.0000177325.47629.4c.

70. Lee, I., Salman, A., & Tal, A., "Gaza protests: 17 Palestinians killed in confrontations with Israeli forces," *CNN*, March 30, 2018, https://edition.cnn.com/2018/03/30/middleeast/gaza-protests-intl/index.html.

71. Lunden, J., "'OSLO' tells the surprising story behind a his-

toric handshake," *NPR*, August 6, 2016, https://www.npr.org/2016/08/06/488737544/oslo-tells-the-surprising-story-behind-a-historic-handshake.

72. Lynch, M., & Telhami, S., "Biden says he will listen to experts. Here is what scholars of the Middle East think," *Brookings*, February 19, 2021, https://www.brookings.edu/blog/order-from-chaos/2021/02/19/biden-says-he-will-listen-to-experts-here-is-what-scholars-of-the-middle-east-think/.

73. Mahdawi, A., "The adultification of children has consequences from Palestine to the US," *The Guardian*, May 21, 2024, https://www.theguardian.com/commentisfree/article/2024/may/04/adultification-children-palestine-us.

74. Masarwa, L., "Sheikh Raed Salah: 'I head to prison standing by my values,'" *Middle East Eye*, August 17, 2020, https://www.middleeasteye.net/news/palestinian-sheikh-raed-salah-prison-israel-jerusalem-al-aqsa-interview.

75. McCausland, B. P., "Illegal New York synagogue tunnel leads to 9 arrests," *BBC News*, January 10, 2024, https://www.bbc.com/news/world-us-canada-67938683.

76. McGowan, J., "Greta Thunberg's stand with Gaza is a problem for the climate change movement," *Forbes*, October 27, 2023, https://www.forbes.com/sites/jonmcgowan/2023/10/25/greta-thunbergs-stand-with-gaza-is-a-problem-for-the-climate-change-movement/.

77. Moussa, E., "Gaza's Christian minority: Israel's unseen victims," *The New Arab*, December 21, 2021, https://www.newarab.com/analysis/gazas-christian-minority-israels-unseen-victims.

78. Muaddi, Q., "2023 is 'deadliest year' for a child in occupied West Bank," *The New Arab*, October 6, 2023, https://www.newarab.com/news/2023-deadliest-year-child-occupied-west-bank.

79. Murphy, M., "Israel, Hamas accused of war crimes in new UN report," *BBC News*, June 12, 2024, https://www.bbc.com/news/articles/cl55gzp7vn9o.

80. Museums Association, "Unesco verifies damage to 43 cultural heritage sites in Gaza," *Museums Association*, April 23, 2024, https://www.museumsassociation.org/museums-journal/news/2024/04/unesco-verifies-damage-to-43-cultural-heritage-sites-in-gaza/.

81. Narea, N., & Samuel, S., "How to think through allegations of genocide in Gaza," *Vox*, November 13, 2023, https://www.vox.com/world-politics/2023/11/13/23954731/genocide-israel-gaza-palestine.

82. Nassar, M. (n.d.)., "The Gaza Strip – why the history of the densely populated enclave is key to understanding the current conflict," *The Conversation*, October 10, 2023, https://theconversation.com/the-gaza-strip-why-the-history-of-the-densely-populated-enclave-is-key-to-understanding-the-current-conflict-215306.

83. Nuki, P., "How Benjamin Netanyahu empowered Hamas. . . and broke Israel," *The Telegraph*, October 17, 2023, https://www.telegraph.co.uk/world-news/2023/10/16/how-benjamin-netanyahu-empowered-hamas/.

84. Obeidat, I. Y. J. B. a. S., "West Bank: Israel Defense Forces accused of possible war crime," *BBC News*, May 2, 2024, https://www.bbc.com/news/articles/cw07wgrwzywo.

85. Omer, A., "Israeli peace activists are more anguished than ever – in a movement that has always been diverse and divided, with differing visions of 'peace,'" *The Conversation*, March 4, 2024, https://theconversation.com/israeli-peace-activists-are-more-anguished-than-ever-in-a-movement-that-has-always-been-diverse-and-divided-with-differing-visions-of-peace-223273.

86. Oppmann, P., "Fidel Castro survived 600 assassination attempts, officials say," *CNN*, November 2016, https://edition.cnn.

com/2016/08/12/americas/cuba-fidel-castro-at-90-after-assassi-
nation-plots/index.html.

87. Ott, H.. "Hamas says Israeli airstrike kills 3 sons of the group's
political leader Ismail Haniyeh in Gaza," *CBS News*, April 10, 2024,
https://www.cbsnews.com/news/hamas-israel-war-ismail-hani-
yeh-sons-killed-gaza-strike/.

88. Palumbo-Liu, D., "What MLK Actually Thought About Israel
and Palestine," *Jacobin*, February 10, 2019, https://jacobin.
com/2019/02/martin-luther-king-israel-palestine-occupation.

89. Perelman, M., "PNI leader Mustafa Barghouti: 'The real goal
is to eradicate the Palestinian people,'" *France 24*, May 2, 2024,
https://www.france24.com/en/tv-shows/t%C3%   AAte-%C3%
A0-t%C3%   AAte/20240205-mustafa-barghouti-the-real-israe-
li-goal-is-to-eradicate-the-palestinian-people.

90. Pew, "Chapter 2: Religious commitment," *Pew Research
Center*, August 9, 2012, https://www.pewresearch.org/reli-
gion/2012/08/09/the-worlds-muslims-unity-and-diversity-2-reli-
gious-commitment/.

91. Prashad, V., "Every place in Gaza—Including Schools—Is a target,"
CounterPunch.org, August 15, 2024, https://www.counterpunch.
org/2024/08/16/every-place-in-gaza-including-schools-is-a-tar-
get/.

92. Shmitd, R., "Prayers go on: Gazans gather beneath toppled
mosques," *NBC News*, June 11, 2015, https://www.nbcnews.com/
storyline/middle-east-unrest/prayers-go-gazans-gather-beneath-
toppled-mosques-n182081.

93. PressTV, "Israeli forces kill four Palestinians in Gaza, occupied
West Bank," *PressTV*, September 19, 2023, https://www.presstv.
ir/Detail/2023/09/19/711170/Palestine-Gaza-al-Aqsa-Youssef-Sa-
lem-.

94. Progler Y., "Drug addiction in Gaza and the illicit trafficking of tramadol," *J Res Med Sci.*, 185-8. PMID: 21526079, May 15, 2010, https://www.ncbi.nlm.nih.gov/pmc/articles/PMC3082799/.

95. Project Decolonise, "Archive footage reveals Israeli settler children's racist songs on school bus," *YouTube*, August 12, 2023, 0:1:04, https://www.youtube.com/watch?v=sDepqjGq0yo.

96. Policy and Service Research, *Public Opinion Poll No (82)*, December 11, 2021, https://www.pcpsr.org/en/node/866.

97. Rassbach, E., "An interview with Dr. Mustafa Barghouti," *CounterPunch.org*, April 18, 2012, https://www.counterpunch.org/2012/04/18/an-interview-with-dr-mustafa-barghouti/.

98. Report, T., "We are just waiting to die: Songs of death, despair from Gazans on the ground," *The Business Standard*, October 25, 2023, https://www.tbsnews.net/hamas-israel-war/we-are-just-waiting-die-songs-death-despair-gazans-ground-726414.

99. Rice, J., ("'My goal is not to have a dialogue; my goal is to solve this madness,'" *Sojourners*, December 14, 2023, https://sojo.net/magazine/january-2024/my-goal-not-have-dialogue-my-goal-solve-madness.

100. Robbins, C. P., "The dilemma of Gaza's Christians," *The New Yorker*, January 24, 2024, https://www.newyorker.com/news/news-desk/the-dilemma-of-gazas-christians.

101. Romo, V., "Doctors are among the many dead in Gaza. These are their stories," *NPR*, November 16, 2023, https://www.npr.org/2023/11/16/1213307710/gaza-doctors-al-shifa-hospital.

102. Roth, A., "Hamas names Yahya Sinwar, architect of 7 October attack, as new leader," *The Guardian*, August 7, 2024, https://www.theguardian.com/world/article/2024/aug/06/hamas-yahya-sinwar-new-leader.

103.   Rubin, S & Soroka, L., "Israel's military, worn down by Gaza, looks warily toward war in Lebanon," *The Washington Post*, July 15, 2024, https://www.washingtonpost.com/world/2024/07/15/israel-lebanon-hezbollah-war-border/.

104.   Sa'di, A. H., "Catastrophe, Memory and Identity: Al-Nakbah as a Component of Palestinian Identity," *Israel Studies, 7(2), 175–198*, 2002, http://www.jstor.org/stable/30245590.

105.   Salem, H., & Salem, H., "Netanyahu Backtracks on Election Pledge to Refuse a Two-State Solution After Sharp Words from the US," *VICE*, July 29, 2024, https://news.vice.com/article/us-says-it-will-re-evaluate-approach-to-israeli-palestinian-conflict-after-netanyahu-election-win.

106.   Sanger, A., "The contemporary law of blockade and the Gaza Freedom Flotilla," *Springer Nature Link*, 2011, https://doi.org/10.1007/978-90-6704-811-8_14.

107.   Sawafta, A., "Poll shows rise in support by Palestinians for armed struggle," *Reuters*, June 13, 2024, https://www.reuters.com/world/middle-east/poll-shows-rise-support-armed-struggle-by-palestinians-2024-06-13/.

108.   Shephardson, C., "Palestinian Christians and Muslims have lived together in the region for centuries – and several were killed recently while sheltering in the historic Church of Saint Porphyrius," *The Conversation*, October 30, 2023, https://theconversation.com/palestinian-christians-and-muslims-have-lived-together-in-the-region-for-centuries-and-several-were-killed-recently-while-sheltering-in-the-historic-church-of-saint-porphyrius-216335.

109.   Springs, A., "Voters support the U.S. calling for permanent ceasefire in Gaza and conditioning military aid to Israel," *Data for Progress*, February 27, 2024, https://www.dataforprogress.org/blog/2024/2/27/voters-support-the-us-calling-for-permanent-ceasefire-in-gaza-and-conditioning-military-aid-to-israel.

110. Staff, M., "Forensic Architecture probe concludes Israeli tank likely killed Palestinian child Hind Rajab," *Middle East Eye*, June 23, 2024, https://www.middleeasteye.net/news/forensic-architecture-probe-says-israeli-tank-fire-likely-killed-palestinian-child-hind-rajab.

111. Strzyżyńska, W., Cousins, R., Amitrano, A., & Sherwood, H., "Doctors, poets, families, babies: victims of Israel's war on Gaza," *The Guardian*, October 24, 2023, https://www.theguardian.com/world/2023/oct/23/doctors-poets-families-babies-victims-of-israels-war-on-gaza.

112. Surkes, S., "Israeli population growth slowing as fertility rates continue to fall – report," *Times of Israel*, January 22, 2024, https://www.timesofisrael.com/israeli-population-growth-slowing-as-fertility-rates-continue-to-fall-report/.

113. Taheri, M., "Full list of countries who voted to give Palestine new UN power," *Newsweek*, May 12, 2024, https://www.newsweek.com/full-list-countries-voted-give-palestine-un-power-1899399.

114. Tass., "Over 70% of Palestinians support Hamas' armed resistance against Israel — poll," *TASS*, December 14, 2023, https://tass.com/world/1721349.

115. The National, "Gazans serve up street food for hundreds forced to flee homes," *The National*, October 19, 2023, https://www.thenationalnews.com/uae/2023/10/19/gazans-serve-up-street-food-for-hundreds-forced-to-flee-homes/.

116. The Listening Post, "The unravelling of the New York Times 'Hamas rape' story," *Al Jazeera*, March 2, 2024, 0:24:51, https://www.aljazeera.com/program/the-listening-post/2024/3/2/the-unraveling-of-the-new-york-times-hamas-rape-story.

117. Fischbach, M., "The West Bank and Gaza: A population profile," *PRB*, April 2002, https://www.prb.org/resources/the-west-bank-and-gaza-a-population-profile/.

118.   Sheehan, D., "These are the poets and writers who have been killed in Gaza," *Literary Hub*, April 29, 2024, https://lithub.com/these-are-the-poets-and-writers-who-have-been-killed-in-gaza/.

119.   Times of India, "Who is Zaher Jabarin, the 'CEO' of Hamas?" *The Times of India*, January 4, 2024, https://timesofindia.indiatimes.com/world/middle-east/who-is-zaher-jabarin-the-ceo-of-hamas/articleshow/106551337.cms.

120.   Tulner, A., "Peace only possible with a 'three-state solution': The Hussein Plan," *Modern Diplomacy*, January 27, 2024, https://moderndiplomacy.eu/2024/01/28/peace-only-possible-with-a-three-state-solution-the-hussein-plan/.

121.   Vincent, I., & Weinthal, B., "Hamas leaders worth staggering $11B revel in luxury — while Gaza's people suffer," *New York Post*, November 7, 2023, https://nypost.com/2023/11/07/news/hamas-leaders-worth-11bn-live-luxury-lives-in-qatar/.

122.   Vincent, I., "Gaza reporter who harbored Israeli hostages at his home wrote for US-based The Palestine Chronicle," *New York Post*, June 17, 2024, https://nypost.com/2024/06/17/world-news/gaza-reporter-abdallah-aljamal-worked-for-us-non-profit/.

123.   Vincent, P. L., "Gaza heritage shield against horror: Plea to Unesco for protection of the monastery," *Telegraph India*, July 20, 2024, https://www.telegraphindia.com/world/gaza-heritage-shield-against-horror-plea-to-unesco-for-protection-of-monastery/cid/2034897.

124.   Besheer, M., "Netanyahu says Rafah offensive will happen with or without cease-fire and hostage release deal," *Voice of America*, May 1, 2024, https://www.voanews.com/a/biden-pledges-cooperation-with-egypt-qatar-to-implement-proposed-israel-hamas-cease-fire/7591462.html.

125.   UN Women: Arab States, "Voices from Gaza: Hala's Journey of Resilience," *UN Women – Arab States*, November 28, 2023, https://

arabstates.unwomen.org/en/stories/feature-story/2023/11/voices-from-gaza-halas-journey-of-resilience-0.

126.   Bushry, A., "Voices of Resilience: Gaza Journalists on the frontlines of truth," *The Edition*, May 3, 2024, https://edition.mv/news/33210.

127.   Arab Center Washington, DC, "Israeli officials' statements on Gaza: Dehumanization and war crimes against Palestinians," *Arab Center Washington DC*, April 29, 2024, https://arabcenterdc.org/resource/israeli-official-statements-on-gaza-dehumanization-and-war-crimes-against-palestinians/.

128.   Sinha, M., "'The Birth of a Nation:'" Who is Nat Turner? | Here & Now," *WBUR.org*, October 7, 2016, https://www.wbur.org/here-andnow/2016/10/07/birth-of-a-nation-nat-turner.

129.   Welsh, C. (n.d.)., "Cache Numismatics," *Cache Historic and World Coins,* accessed November 7, 2024, https://www.cache-coins.org/palestine.htm.

130.   IMF Country Report, "West Bank and Gaza," *IMF Country Report, 2023(327), 1*, 2023, https://doi.org/10.5089/9798400253843.002.

131.   Yasin, B., "Effects of the Israeli blockade on the economic and humanitarian conditions in the Gaza Strip," *Middle East Monitor*, September 12, 2021, https://www.middleeastmonitor.com/20210912-effects-of-the-israeli-blockade-on-the-economic-and-humanitarian-conditions-in-the-gaza-strip/